Bad Pastor

Journey Of A Creative Believer

James A. Bogans III

Bad Pastor

DEDICATION

Of course, I want to dedicate this to my family. To my wife who willingly signed up to do life with me, even when I showed her all of me. There is nothing more beautiful or meaningful to me than you. You believe in me in ways I didn't know extended to human beings. You are the ultimate cheerleader/teacher/therapist (That was an inside joke because I've always had a thing for cheerleaders, teachers and therapists.) I love you and I appreciate you. To my son who showed me parts of myself that I tried to forget. Thank you for being the best part of my memory. To my brother. I joke with people when I say that I grew up with a mother, a father, and a father. It's the absolute truth, though. You were a parent to me when mommy and daddy worked around the clock to provide for us. I once heard you tell Lauren that I do everything better than you. I'm not sure if that's true or not, but if it is it's only because you're who I learned everything from. To mommy who refused to allow quitting to be in our vocabulary. Our family's backbone was built out of Chromium stainless steel because that's how you were forged. Everything our family stands on came from your work, prayers and discipline. To daddy who never met a hard heart he couldn't soften. You led our home with such passion, strength and love that I didn't know if I could marry someone who loved as well as you do.

There are 3 families, that I would also like to dedicate this to. That is the Stancil family, the Noland family and the Cross family. At the earliest and rawest stages of my creativity, your love, support and acknowledgement were catalysts to me becoming who I am today. You treated me as your own. You protected me when I didn't know how to protect myself. And you built space in your lives for me when you didn't have to. You showed me how to work, how to love, how to forgive, how to be loyal and how to accept. So, Cecil, Hattie, Kelli, Philip thank you. Mike, Kathy, Brittany, Jeff, Brandon, Joshua thank you. Big Joe, Tammy, Joe-Joe, Halle, Benjamin thank you.

As a creative, our life force is wrapped in inspiration and the cultivation of it. To the three people who cultivated the most creative parts of me, thank you. Ms. Pohutsky, as a 5th grade transfer, I came to your class lost with no direction. I'm not sure if you meant to but you opened something inside of me that I depend on every day. You opened my love for words and poetry. You're the reason I read the dictionary, you and Malcolm X. You're also the reason I continue to write, and to quote the poet you had me memorize, "The woods are lovely, dark and deep but I have promises to keep and miles to go before I sleep and miles to go before I sleep." Michael Danners, you taught me how to create. You exemplify the very freedom one must have to truly tap into becoming the creator one desires to be and you selflessly gave that to me. You showed me how to bring something into existence, free from the burden of outside perception. That's a freedom most people may never get to experience. Shawneda Crout, you taught me creative control. I knew how to write, and I knew how to create, but I had no idea how to organize and discipline what I was creating nor my creativity. You gave me that by allowing me to witness your unconventional structured genius. What I am as a creator is largely due to the three of your contributions to my life. I thank you and love you all.

Bad Pastor

FOREWORD

By Dr. Marquise Gold

The day we were born, I know for a fact that none of us knew what we were getting ourselves into. We didn't know the family we were entering; we didn't know the homes we would live in, and we sure didn't know the path that we would take. Some say the path is selected for us in advance and others say that we get to select the path ourselves. For whichever one is true, I can't say for sure that I selected the path to become a pastor. You know we live in a world where gifts enter our universe everyday through birthing. However, there are rare gifts that enter the earth that stand out and are completely different. They are special, unique and powerful. The individuals with these gifts receive such a great portion of power that they're often known by their gift alone. It's the blessing and the curse. No one starts out at the top of their game no matter what industry you work in. Most of who we become after we are born is mixed with our natural talents plus trial & error. Our mistakes while on the path towards destiny and purpose serve as our greatest teacher, if we allow them to. When you look back over your life you will soon realize that everything is interconnected.

We will all experience birth and death. However, very few will experience anointing. To be anointed and gifted comes with tremendous paths lined with discovery, trauma, success, pain and cycles. None of these are unavoidable for the anointed. It's what marks you even when you don't ask for it.

Once your anointing is discovered then it is your job to become determined, no matter how hard the path is. This book reminds us of how everything in our life is pointing us in a direction that will ultimately get us to our destination even if we become lost. James, who is also my brother uniquely paints a picture in this book by using his life experiences to render to us that no matter what we go through, it all works together for good. I'm proud of my brother because he shows many of us that you can withstand and survive life's crippling situations by being BAD at whatever you do. You were born for this. You were anointed for this. And you must be determined for this.

I hope you find inspiration and strength while reading this book. Allow James to take you on a journey that even he didn't realize was all interconnected to lead him to where he is now.

CONTENTS

INTRODUCTION

I was supposed to finish this book months earlier. I had my deadline locked in and everything, but then my wife happened. She pulled me aside as I was finishing what I thought was the final chapters of the book, and she told me that she'd been watching me. She told me that it looked like I was focusing so hard on finishing the book that I stopped writing it. I stopped feeling it. It was becoming a task that I just wanted to be done with. She's always had a gift for noticing things about me far before I catch onto them myself. She was right. My deadline was eight days away and I began counting words rather than writing them.

My wife, Curnesia, sent me a book that she started reading and told me to read it. The book was called "Balance" by Touré Roberts. When the pandemic started, we had this running inside joke that he was our new pastor. It's an inside joke, you don't have to get it. I still remember what I said to myself when I saw it. "Hmmph, looks interesting. I'll read it once I finish these last few chapters of my book." A few days went by, and I hadn't written one word of my book. That's because I was consumed with reading "Balance". It was like the book spoke to every part of what I was going through at the time. I'm a creative artist working on my music and film projects. I have a media ideation & production company that needs tending to. I'm training to become a better public speaker. I have a wife and a five-year-old son who are my priority. And now I'm in the middle of my first year as a pastor, a job that often feels like I'm doing pretty bad at. Oh yeah, and I'm writing a book. My balance was off, and I didn't realize it until my wife stopped me from moving. I'm a fast reader so it took me a few days to finish reading the book, and when I was done it felt like a brand-new energy hit my body. It not only changed my outlook on my productivity, but it also gave me perspective on what I'd be writing about. My initial goal was to write a book on my first year as a lead pastor. Yet, with my new, fresh and balanced perspective, I realized that I couldn't tell that story without giving context of how I got here.

My entire life has been about art, entertainment and production. So as a creative I always want to push the envelope. I love to create, and I love to change. When an update pops up on my phone, I press 'confirm' without even thinking. Exploring the newness of something breathes life into me. I just didn't know that the world I was now ignorantly stepping into would categorize that as unstable. Throughout the decades, we've witnessed just about everything change. Music has gone from bulky 12" records to formless sound bytes of streaming. Movies went from being in black and white to a 4D VR experience. Transportation is even changing from gas fuel to electric. Yet, one thing I've had a hard time seeing a change in is church, the black church specifically. For a community birthed out of the protest of slavery in 1787, not seeing or feeling much of a change in it is not only alarming but scary. Every now and then there would be a jolt to the system. A disrupter would show up and shock us with a new perspective. Kirk Franklin would come out with "Stomp". Or Tyler Perry would teach through Madea. We'd marvel at it and even begin to incorporate elements of it into our church services. After a while, though, we would slip right back into business as usual 'Church'. This stale, changeless existence that's protected by our religious masses by calling it tradition has always vexed me. I'm not sure exactly what my role is in this next wave of disturbance, but I'm pretty sure tradition is out of the window.

If anything, I wanted to write this to let certain people know that they were seen. For those who spent the better parts of their lives being angry at God because you were angry at people, I see you. For those who never felt like you had a place in the church because you weren't like them, I see you. For those whose creative perspective didn't fit the mold of the building, I see you. For those who have been screaming at the top of your souls to be seen as human and not sinner, I see you. For those who love God but find it difficult to love people, I see you. For those whose love was trampled over, and hearts molested by a poor excuse for what we call a 'Christian', I see you. For those who just want something to believe in and want to be believed in, I see you.

1. HOW DID WE GET HERE?

How in the fuck did I become a pastor? If "unqualified for the position" needed a face for the definition, it would borrow mine. Let's go down the list. Bible College, no. Seminary, nope. Baptist, Cogic, evangelical, Pentecostal, nondenominational... none of it. Church culture, oblivious. Ability to speak in tongues, nonexistent. When you think of a pastor by any stretch of the imagination, I'm just not what you think of. Now, I've only allotted myself fifteen cuss words for the duration of this book and I'm afraid I'm going to use all of them in the first chapter. As I write this, as you read this, pray for me. Or just judge me. Whichever makes you feel better.

My name is James Artis Bogans III. I am a husband. A father. A brother. A son, an artist. A writer. An audio engineer. A sound tech. A Filmmaker. A rapper. And a pastor. I'm so many other things, but these are the ones that I consciously connect with my purpose in life the most. On January 1st, 2022, I sat at my computer preparing my first sermon as lead pastor of Fresh Start Church. I was reflecting and trying to figure out how I got there. I thought maybe that would help me figure out the purpose for me being here in this office and the title of Pastor. If I'm being truthful, I never wanted this position. I never wanted this title. I would much rather live in a world where I could affect change in people without them knowing who I was. Do not get me wrong, I love talking to people but I'm more comfortable facilitating conversations. I love being an artist, but I'm more comfortable being a producer. I love being a performer, but I'm more comfortable being an engineer. I love teaching, but I'm more comfortable being the student. All my life I have been behind the scenes, and I was happy with my greatest accomplishments hiding behind someone else's glory. I preferred it that way. It's been made apparent, as of late, that God does not share my preference.

Now to my reflection. Anytime I reflect, I enter myself into my own personal time machine and investigate myself. I attach myself to a detail or event and then follow the emotion tethered to it from past and future events. I call them Time Trips. I'm going to be taking you on these Time Trips to give you context behind why I'm such a bad pastor. Not bad as in bad or bad as in good, but bad as in not the standard of what one may think it's supposed to be. We live in a world where many people believe themselves to have open minds when their minds are limited to their experiences, and most people don't experience much of a variety. Each Time Trip I take you on will give color to an otherwise black and white ideal. Those who don't know me will feel like we've known each other forever. And those who do know me may feel like we've never known each other at all. Enjoy the ride.

THURSDAY NOVEMBER 14, 1991

Growing up, I've always had asthma and it has consistently landed me in the hospital more than three times a year in my childhood. One time, I was five years old, and I was in the hospital again for asthma. After a few days, I got better, and I was allowed to go home. I had a check-up a little while after and the doctor, my doctor at the time, told my parents that she wanted to put me on Ritalin after wanting to diagnose me with ADD, now called ADHD, along with some sort of spectrum of autism.

Lack of eye contact, speech delay, socially awkward... She ran through a list of things she noticed from me to back up her hypothesis. Mommy didn't say anything. She just stared at the doctor, listening with intent. But then again, she didn't have to say much. Daddy did all the talking that time. He was really upset, and I don't remember everything he said to my doctor. I do, however, remember one phrase. "I will burn this whole motherfucking Hospital down." Before I knew it, we were outside of the doctor's office.

As we were walking to the bus stop all I remember daddy saying is, "ain't nothing wrong with my son, Tresie. Ain't nothing wrong with James." I didn't know it then, but the fear that he must have felt in that very moment must have been polarizing. To find out that the being that you brought into the world may very well be much different than everyone else, or the shame behind fathering someone with a condition you used to make fun of in school, changes perspective. Surprisingly, mommy didn't say much, but I do remember her saying "Jimmy we are going to work with him."

I only remember the story in fragments. More than remembering the events that happened, I remember how I felt while it was happening. I say that because throughout most of my childhood I spent a lot of time trying to fit in, not knowing, in full, how different I was. I was never told how or why I was different. I was not even told that I was different. It was never explained to me, as if it never existed. There was never a discussion, not until I became an adult.

At an early age. I learned the skill of blending in and becoming invisible. In almost every room I was in, I was physically the biggest person. Yet, I was invisible. That was intentional because I didn't want anyone to know I was different, even though I was not sure what that difference was. I needed time to learn the patterns and social constructs of the people in front of me. There was no way I could become a normal person, but with time, I learned how to act like one. Every new social interaction I had, I was quiet. I listened, I watched. I picked up on social cues, inflections, types of speech, comedy and seriousness. I learned so much so that the next time we had this social interaction, I could blend in. I could do what they do. Say what they say. Act like they act. Become invisible.

PRESENT

I did the invisible thing for school. I did it for family functions. I did it for organized sports, and it was easy. Yet what I could never do it with was church. Since I was a little kid, I have always had a serious discomfort with church. I could never explain it, but something about it has never sat well with me. I never had the words for it until now. Thank God for daddy who gave us a choice every single Sunday. He said, "you can either go to church with your mother. Or you can stay home and watch football with me." Mark went to church with mommy. I stayed home and watched football. Even though I stayed home with daddy, I usually ended up reading some book or playing a video game.

God and Satan had their hooks in me deep and were doing some serious work on me as a kid. Satan wanted what I saw in church to keep me away from it. God wanted me to pay attention to what I saw and talk to Him about it. I struggled to stay invisible in church because the things that made me different also made me unique. And it is not hubris when I say that the things that make me unique are the things that make me necessary in this space. That only took 36 years to figure out.

We all yearn to be unique until we understand what that really means in its completion. The loneliness that ensues along with the misunderstanding of others, especially those closest to you is a part of it. I am different.

I don't mean in the cultural sense or reciting a 2 Chainz song. I mean that I am not like you or anyone, for that matter. I'm left-handed. That's 10% of the population. I struggle with dyslexia. That's 20% of the population. I struggle with ADHD, which is 7% of the population. Social anxiety is also 7% of the population. I have an IQ of 137. That's 2% of the population. My blood type is ab negative, 1 percent of the population. I'm over 6 feet tall, 15% of the population. My Myers-Briggs personality trait is an INFJ, that's 1.5% of the population. My Enneagram personality trait is a type five, which is 5% of the population. Don't forget that I am a black American and that is .00553% of the population. Using those attributes alone, of all 8 billion people in the world there are about 7,856 people that are similar to me. That's 40 people per country if spread evenly. To be quite literal, I am one of a kind and it has only taken 36 years for me to be able to accept that as an asset. Again, this is not hubris. This is just a demonstration that we only get to be unique when we can recognize and accept the things that make us different.

People sought to be the kind of different I am, while I was trying to be more like them. I saw so many people trying to be different for the sake of being different, yet I was trying to fit in because I didn't like the things that made me different. This is something I battled with back and forth, close to my whole life. I won some. I lost some. Somehow, those wins and losses landed me here.

SATURDAY DECEMBER 7, 2002

I didn't start going to church willfully until I was close to 17 years old. I went with my brother on a Saturday to a church he was attending. I rode with him because he had a meeting. I figured no one would be there so I had no problem going. To my surprise, the building we went into was full of people, teenagers. They were rehearsing for something they called "Friday Night Live". It's a talent show made for the youth of the church. While we were there, I met Kelli, Chris, Marcus, Terrence, Paul, Keyona, Philip and Travys. Most of which I'm still in contact with today, but it was this group of people that hooked me into coming back to the church the next day for Sunday morning service.

I sat in service with this same group of people while the choir was singing. The same feeling I always got while in church, I felt there too. But I looked around at these new friends I just made a day ago. They were singing and dancing the same way everyone else was in the church. I thought to myself, "maybe I'm trippin'. If they're all ok with this. Why can't I?" As I said before, I was good at blending in and becoming invisible. I ignored what I felt. The feeling that I couldn't explain started coming less and less as I suppressed it. I learned how to sing and how to dance along with everyone else. It took a few weeks, but I was able to blend in, become invisible. Not invisible in the sense of not being seen, but in the sense that when they saw me, they saw everyone else.

This lasted for months. I participated in the talent shows. I joined the step team and attended youth church. I became a regular and I was great at playing the part. I met some great people while doing it, too. Even though I was still unmoved when it came to the church services and sermons, I knew if I could control this mysterious feeling I had, I would be ok in the crowd. I fit in and fitting in felt good, regardless of how it happened. I don't know if it's unfortunate or fortunate, but it didn't last.

During my time with the step team, I became very close with our coach, Darrick Fitzgerald. He believed in strict discipline, excellence and a word I tend to use quite often now, humanity. I'm not sure why, but he took to me the same way I took to him. It was almost as if he could see me thinking and was intrigued to know what I was thinking about. Not to judge it, as so many others did, but to assess and cultivate it. Aside from my parents and my brother, no one had been that interested in my thoughts. Before and after step practice we'd meet up and share thoughts about any and everything. Music, art, politics, science, thinking, everything. I had never had a mentor before, but I assume that's what it felt like.

We were approaching the end of our last practice before our first step show when Darrick announced he'd be leaving the step team. We all pushed for an explanation, but he just said that he and the church came to an agreement for him to leave. Half of the team felt abandoned by him. Another half ended up quitting, but a few of us were not taking his answer lying down. We pushed for more answers and thanks to the investigative skills of a great friend, Kelli, we found out something.

Darrick wasn't quitting, he was being pushed out by church leadership. Darrick was engaged to be married in a few months. He and his fiancé were living together and according to church leadership, that was unacceptable. I didn't come from church politics, so I didn't know the rules, but they called it shacking. Thinking back, I wondered if there was more to the story. At the time, we didn't care, we wanted our coach back, so we protested. A handful of us launched our teenage crusade to get our coach back. We ultimately failed to get him back on the team, but this crusade of ours would ensure that I'd never be able to be invisible again, no matter how hard I'd try.

During our protest, we decided to use the very book that was used to teach us every week, The Bible. That would be the first time I would ever open The Bible for myself. I still remember my first thoughts upon reading it for the first time... "What the fuck? This is not the shit they teach us in youth church." It may have taken me a few weeks to get through the whole thing, about the same amount of time as it took me to get through the dictionary. One of the perks of ADHD is an obsession to finish what you start by obsessively hyper focusing on that one thing.

A side effect is that I didn't do my homework or any schoolwork for those three weeks. I almost failed chemistry because of those three weeks.

Needless to say, I stopped attending youth church and youth Bible study for a while. I felt hopeless. I felt injustice. And after reading the Bible, I felt anger. When we were protesting, countless adults told us to stop, stay in a child's place. All except for Coach Miller. For some reason, he always had our backs. I honestly think he was getting a kick out of our rebellion. Either way, I personally appreciated his support. The other adults even referenced scripture out of context to make their point to us. We were chastised to let it go, and because we weren't armed with enough information, we let it go. We were teenagers and we felt powerless so I grabbed hold of the only weapon I could wield, rebellion. If church was a place of community, forgiveness and lack of judgment, then what were we doing? That feeling that I was suppressing for so long began imploding inside of me. Something didn't sit right. But, as usual, I said to myself, "maybe it's just me. Maybe I'm trippin'."

SUNDAY JANUARY 4, 2004

I was at the brink of being checked out of church altogether when one day they announced that special Bible study classes would be offered on Wednesday nights, the regular night for Bible study. I looked at the list of classes and I came across apologetics. In my head I said, "Yeah this church owes me an apology for being hypocrites!" That was my teenage rebellion talking. The name looked cool enough to pique my interest. Plus, I had extra motivation for taking the class. A girl that I liked was taking it too. I didn't know it then, but the class would open up something in me that I would never be able to close. Apologetics is not saying I'm sorry. It means to argue in defense of. The class was designed to teach us the origin, foundation and backbone of our faith in order to defend it in gentle confidence. Our instructor, Leroy Lamar III, did just that. It has been twenty years and I still remember every class he taught us. That's how open I was. The information was great by itself, but the way he taught it to us fed a hunger inside of me that I had no idea was even there.

That caused me to study more. It caused me to search more. It also caused a chasm between this new but already fragile relationship with church. The apologetics classes were on Wednesdays. Church was on Sundays. I'd learn something on Sunday just to have it contradicted on Wednesday. Not everything, but enough for me to not know what to trust. I still never said anything. After all, these people had been doing this for years. I'd only been there a few months. What could I have possibly known that they didn't? These thoughts of mine kept my mouth quiet yet my eyes and ears were open.

The class lasted eight weeks and we were back to regular Bible study, to my dismay. My brother convinced me to go back to youth Bible study. He couldn't take me to the young adult classes with him anymore. I didn't mind too much. Many of my step teammates were there also and I was in the beginning stages of finding my voice, something I wasn't quite familiar with. The only problem with it was my voice sounded more like questions than anything. I'd question everything in class. Between my personal studies in apologetics and what I'd hear in Sunday service, youth Bible study was more confusing than challenging. My questions would not only irritate the teacher, but my fellow teenagers as well. I even heard someone under their breath say, "shut up. He asks too many questions."

SATURDAY MARCH 15, 1997

I'd been playing baseball since I was six years old. I loved the sport. The balance of athleticism and intellect kept me occupied, engaged and happy. I played for four years at Carroll Park while my family lived in Baltimore. I won contests, participated in all-star games and won countless awards while we were there. I won the Unsung Hero Trophy and the Golden Glove Trophy for the league I was in. I was up for MVP, but I was overlooked. Daddy said it was because of my skin color and because the trophy went to the coach's son. At least that's what I heard him say to mommy. I asked him about it. I said, "Daddy, why didn't I win the MVP? I had better stats all year, more home runs, RBI's and a higher batting average than anyone on the team." I didn't know he was already frustrated about it, especially as assistant coach. That would also mean that his recommendations for MVP were ignored along with my consideration. He said, "I wish y'all would stop asking me that. You ask too many questions." That sentence was all too familiar to me. I'd been hearing it all my life and every time I heard it, it only meant one thing. "Shut up." So, I let it go. Months later we moved to Columbia, Maryland and I couldn't wait for baseball season to come back around. I was excited to continue playing, even though we were in a new city. When it was time to play again, I joined a new team. On a particular Saturday practice, we were doing our normal routines when I noticed one of our outfielders continuously throwing the ball behind the runners. This just means he not only ran the risk of hitting the runner with the ball but also missing the opportunity of a double play, getting two outs in one play. I played first base, so I asked my first base coach, "why does he keep throwing behind the runner?" My first base coach shook his head and said, "don't worry about it, Bogans. Just make sure nobody makes it past first base." I was still curious, though. I wanted to make sure the way I was taught to play was still the right way. I was ok with learning new ways to play, but I was too curious to leave my question unanswered. After practice, I saw my head coach, in baseball we call them managers, walking to his car. I stood there contemplating whether I should ask or not. I'd been wanting to since I first saw it two weeks ago.

"Ask him, James. No, don't ask him. You need to know. It's not that important. What if you're missing something by not asking? It's not worth the trouble. Maybe this is why you didn't win the MVP last year. You don't want to deal with that." Yep, that was my brain. Before I lost my nerve again, I yelled, "Coach!" He turned around, "What's up, Bogans." I walked up to him while looking downward, "hey, is there a reason the outfielders keep throwing behind the runners on base?" I said outfielders, knowing it was just one; Coach knew too. He went off on me. "Maybe you should worry about why you missed the ground ball in the 7th. Let me worry about Mason." I wouldn't find out until later that Mason was Coach's nephew and he was on the team because Coach promised his sister he could be on the team. He slammed his trunk, and I could hear him muttering, "ask too many fucking questions." I knew what that meant... "Shut up." That is exactly what I did. I also never played baseball again. I guess the church isn't the only place where leadership penalizes others for their own inability to correct a problem. Unfortunately, I allowed that to stop me from playing a sport that I loved, a sport that gave me a place to belong.

WEDNESDAY APRIL 7, 2004

I had stopped talking in youth Bible study for a few weeks now. I spent most of my time daydreaming about music and rap lyrics to keep myself from speaking. During class, I was writing rap lyrics for a song called "Watch Me". I had been writing and rewriting it for weeks. I was so consumed with the song that I didn't see him come through the door. "James, you got a verse for me? Or can we learn about Jesus together?" Everyone laughed. I looked up uninterested only to recognize that I missed the part where our youth pastor told us we had a guest speaker that day. It was Darrick Fitzgerald, my former step team coach. My posture changed. No offense to anyone else, but I felt like today I was going to learn something worth learning. I smiled, "My bad, Unc, keep going." He wrote on the board one of the longest words I had ever seen. The word was 'latitudinarian'. The class spent about 20 minutes trying to guess what it meant. The only clue he gave was that he wanted us to become latitudinarians. There were plenty of Bibles in the classroom, but no dictionaries so we spent another 10 minutes guessing until he told us. A latitudinarian is someone allowing latitude in religion, showing no preference among varying creeds and forms of worship. He continued giving us other definitions to help everyone understand when he landed on something so simple yet seldom utilized. "I don't want to teach you all to be ministers or priests. I just want to teach you to be thinkers, free thinkers." I looked around to see a mixture of blank faces and a few that looked how I would imagine myself looking; engaged. "They can't possibly know he's teaching us this," I thought to myself. At the end of our class, Darrick was leaving early so he could make it to the bookstore he managed before Bible study was over. Walking out the door, he turned to us and asked, "raise your hand. How many of you believe you would die for God?" Everyone raised their hand. "That's easy. Now, try living for Him." He walked out.

2. MAYBE YOU'RE IN THE WRONG PLACE

SUNDAY JUNE 10, 2007

I found it a bit ironic that the next meaningful memory I had of church came 3 years after the last one, ranking me in the stereotypical statistic of young adults abandoning and leaving the church after high school. When I arrived, I was hit with a barrage of questions. 'Where have you been? What happened? You been out here sinning?' I have been told that I'm pretty good at ignoring people and since I don't remember answering anyone, I assume that's what I did. To be quite honest though, my actual answers were too long to speak about in passing. How was I supposed to explain that I spent the last year on a tour to every strip club in Atlanta trying to break a record on radio while having trouble reconciling my place in the world and how that differs from my place in the church? The last person I said that to only heard the word strip club. Who was I supposed to tell that I felt church to be less and less necessary because I began finding it very similar to school? The last person I told that to just told me that I better get into a good college. And who in the church was I going to tell that I spent the last few months getting over my bad breakup by entertaining as many women as I could stand to be around? We all know how the church feels about sex. Let's just pretend it doesn't exist, while at the same time prepare for the baby dedication next week. Yeah, I just ignored the questions and headed to my seat. I remember sitting in the back row of the first section on the right side of the church. I remember because it was the first time I had ever gone to church on my own. I didn't ride with my brother. I wasn't with my friends I met years before. No parents, no girlfriend, no step team mates. It was my first time doing this on my own. Twenty years old and that was the first time I had ever gone to church by myself.

I don't remember what songs were sung. I don't remember who was around me. I don't even remember what the pastor was talking about. All I remember is being doubled over crying in my seat. I could hear people around me whispering. "What's wrong with him?" "He crying." "He caught the holy ghost." To be clear, I didn't. I was frustrated. I was a twenty-year-old overwhelmed college dropout whom nothing was going right for at the time. I was no longer with my rap group, lost a relationship, lost two friendships and two jobs I was on the verge of losing. All of the emotion came flooding out of me.

MONDAY DECEMBER 29, 1997

Emotion was always tough for me. Not because I couldn't control it, but because I could control it all too well. So well that, at times, I had forgotten how to feel them. As a kid, controlling it was much harder. My family wasn't the best with emotion. Uncles, aunts, grandparents, cousins; we all handled emotion by fighting or lashing out. When I was little, daddy would always say that I had my mommy's anger. I never understood what he meant until this moment.

It was a few days after Christmas, and I was in our living room of 9757 Clocktower Lane apartment 203. I was playing with my new toys and watching cartoons on TV. As a huge wrestling fan, I had developed quite the collection of action figures. Hulk Hogan, Randy Savage, The Undertaker and Shawn Michaels were some of my favorites, but I just got two new action figures. Stone Cold Steve Austin and The Rock, then named Rocky Maivia. My brother, Mark, didn't like wrestling. He loved music, in particular, Bad Boy Records. He was in our bedroom listening to Biggie's Life After Death, Puff Daddy and The Family's No Way Out and Mase's Harlem World on repeat.

The music was so loud I couldn't hear the TV so I turned it up. Mark came out of our room and said, "James, turn that TV down. I can't hear my music!" He went back into the room and turned the music up. I grabbed the TV remote and turned the volume up. He turned his music up some more and I did the same with the TV. I wasn't even paying attention to the TV; I was just being an annoying little brother trying to get my big brother's attention. I required no one's attention in the world, except my brother's. In a lot of ways, I'm still like that today. He bursted out of the room with lyrics from "Notorious Thugs" blaring from our room and turned the TV off in the living room. I waited until he got back to our bedroom door, and I turned the TV back on with the volume on full blast. I began laughing, I thought it was funny. He didn't. Mark grabbed my Hulk Hogan action figure and threw it at me.

That isn't anything abnormal. He'd start with me, or I'd start with him, we'd argue, throw stuff, maybe even wrestle, that's all I wanted to begin with, and then we'd eat something. But that time when he threw the action figure at me, it hit me square in my throat, taking my breath away and knocking me to the floor. A white fire poured over my body and my anger began swelling until it overwhelmed me. My brother first looked to see if I was ok until he saw the look in my eyes, a look he's seen before. He immediately ran away, and I chased after him screaming at the top of my lungs. He shut our bedroom door and locked it so I wouldn't get in. I banged on the door, kicked it, pushed it and charged into it. I was so angry I began punching the door, yelling for him to let me in. He screamed, "stop before I call daddy!" Our father worked at the apartment complex we lived in so he could be home in minutes if need be. Daddy was always the lenient parent, but one thing he did not tolerate was his two sons fighting one another. Neither of our parents played that. We could rob someone, steal, sell drugs, even murder someone in cold blood and they'd be calm and forgiving about it. But if they ever caught us fighting each other, they'd beat us to a pulp. "You fight them out there! Not each other," they'd always say.

Still breathing hard, I stopped banging on the door. It was too late, though, because I had already bent the door off the hinges creating a loud creaking whenever the door opened. I had lost my temper before, but that time was different. I never recognized the terror in my brother's eyes until then. Even though he would pass it off as laughter, I scared him. I never paid attention to the damage I had done until then. Releasing the anger felt good, hitting things felt good, but realizing the way I was doing it, did not feel good. I went back into the living room and turned the TV off. I sat on the floor pondering the reasons I would lose my temper so recklessly.

I thought about how I saw my parents deal with conflict. Mommy was always the fiery one, short fuse with a meticulous talent for knowing how and where to hurt someone. Daddy was calmer but had his shuddering streaks of meanness with his curt words. I also noticed that those weapons were only deployed when one or both of them were angry, leading me to believe that they had a lack of control when it came to strong emotion, anger in particular. My brother and I were no different. I can't count the number of fights we were in growing up. He was kicked out of school. I've been kicked out of camp. We were kicked out of boy scouts. My entire family, we were the greatest people until we were faced with an emotion that we couldn't handle, anger. About an hour later, my brother came out of the bedroom. At that age, I didn't know how to apologize so I expressed my remorse the only way I knew how. I asked if he wanted to play with my toys with me. He nodded 'no' as he walked to the kitchen. He looked back and asked, "you hungry?" Looking back, that's how we communicated apologies because this is what we saw from our parents. That day at 11 years old, I vowed to teach myself how to handle emotion.

I taught myself well, a little too well, because as time went along, I went from handling emotion to nearly eliminating it altogether. My family would even joke that when I was younger, I had a demon in me when I got angry. I'm not too sure they were joking.

SUNDAY JUNE 10, 2007

Nearly ten years of emotion came out of me that day. Anger, sadness, worry, contempt, joy, love, compassion. I lifted my head to people looking at me and a few offering me tissues. I wiped my eyes with my hands and pretended I didn't see people staring at me. After service was over, I left to go to my car. As I was leaving the building I hear a voice yell, "B-more!" That was one of my nicknames when I was on the step team. I turned back and it was Darrick Fitzgerald. I went over and dapped him up. He didn't ask where I had been. He didn't ask why I hadn't been to church. He just said, "I miss you. We gotta catch up."

And we did. We caught up, but it would still be a while before I made my way back into the church on a regular basis. I would help with events since my brother had become the youth pastor. I even coached the step team for a while. I just couldn't bring myself to go to service. I wasn't hurt by anyone, and I wasn't angry. I was apathetic. I convinced myself it was a me problem, so I kept it to myself. I convinced myself that it was just youthful rebellion. I convinced myself that I needed to be fixed.

A few months later, Darrick hit me up and invited me to his young adult Bible study called FLAVA. I don't remember what the acronym stood for. I do, however, remember he was adamant about calling it young adult and not college ministry. "Not everyone goes to college," he said. "That doesn't mean they can't come." I told him that I would check it out. The only two people who could convince me to participate in anything in church were him and my brother. So I went. I don't know why I was expecting this quintessential classroom style Bible study. I must have been so far removed that I forgot who Darrick was. I walked into the bookstore where Darrick volunteered. It was on the opposite side of the church sanctuary so when I heard the Unwrapped hip-hop jazz music playing, I didn't think anything of it. It was like we were in a coffee shop and for the next 2 hours it was our sanctuary.

When I walked inside, I remember feeling a lack of judgment, a lack of status quoism, a lack of me needing to hide. I didn't ever feel that way unless I'm at home or on stage. Maybe it was because there were only 15 people there. Maybe it was because I already had a relationship with the teacher. Maybe it was because I finally met a few like-minded people. Either way, it felt good to be there. There was me, Ashley, Toya, Santario, Joy, Doneshia, Arlisha, Shaun, Vince, Zony, Joe, Shawn, Anthony. Our instructors were Darrick and Kandice with a guest speaker every now and then. There were others, but we were the regulars. I began going every week. I wasn't going to church on Sunday, but I was going to the FLAVA Bible study every Wednesday.

WEDNESDAY APRIL 9, 2008

There was one week where we had a guest speaker, one of the most creative artists and people I've ever known, Betty Hart. I remembered Betty from my times being in the church services. She sang in the choir next to one of my former step team coaches, Meca. There must have been at least 40 people in the choir, but I only saw them. They were always so expressive and convinced that what they were singing was true. It emitted off them like a beam of light that you couldn't take your eyes off. When Darrick was removed from our step team, it was Meca who took the reins as our step team coach. Under her, we won countless competitions, anchored the growth in youth ministry, and became mini celebrities in that community. She was a no nonsense, respect oriented, excellence driven mother of two great daughters who taught me the importance of disciplined leadership by example.

The best way I could describe Betty is to say that she was a smoldering fire. She was always kind, calm and considerate. Yet, when she stepped onto the stage, any stage, there were flames that launched out of her like targeted missiles aimed at your heart. Darrick knew how to make you think. Betty knew how to make you feel, and feeling was a struggle for me on a consistent basis. As an actress and director, her creativity gave me an excitement I didn't really feel in church.

I can't quite latch onto her exact lesson for that day, but I do remember a question she asked. "What's stopping you?" I loved the way she could ask open ended questions and you knew exactly what she was talking about, even if you wanted to play stupid by asking, "stopping me from doing what?" Before then, I hadn't really been all that vocal in the class. Stage fright, social anxiety and a slight distrust for my own words kept me quiet for a long time. When she asked the question, however, I was the first to speak. "I'm disobedient," I blurted out. "It's like, I know what I'm supposed to be doing and it's just not happening for me." I could feel everyone's eyes weld up at me. Half surprised that I was talking and the other half that I would admit something that vulnerable. I didn't see it that way at the time, I'm not sure if I saw it as anything at all. I just knew that there was something in Betty's teaching and her questions that provoked me to speak. After my answer, everyone else began to speak.

Betty continued teaching, making a point not to fix, coddle or condemn anyone's answer. I didn't realize then, but those answers were more for us than they were for class. Brilliant. After the class was over, Betty came to me and she said, "Maybe it's not happening for you because you're in the wrong place. If I send you something and you're not at the place I sent it, how will you ever get it?" I wouldn't understand the fullness of what she said until years later, but in the present, it still shifts my perspective whenever I'm dealing with conflict.

It was normal for our class to run late. Sometimes, we wouldn't know it was time to end class until we saw people coming out from regular Bible study or youth Bible study. High school students would flood the bookstore expressing how they couldn't wait to graduate so they could come to our class. Adults from regular Bible study would come just to sit in our class. Some were interested, others were just there to audit Darrick. We all knew who was who. That day, however, a great friend and sister to Betty walked in. Tasha Smith. She came and gave me a big hug, "how was class?" She asked. I smiled, "it was good." "And where have you been? You been gone for a while. You ok?" Even though I'd been going to the FLAVA classes, that's the only place I was going in the church. I was still absent for a lot of people. Anyone who knew me knew I hated that question, "where have you been?" Not because of the question, but because of the insinuation behind it when used by church people. Yet, if anyone could ask me that question, it was Tasha. To be clear, I have one mother. I have one father. I have never played the 'that's my play momma or play daddy' games made so popular in church. At that stage in my life, I didn't even have godparents. I say all of that to say, Tasha's like a mother to me. Not in place of my own, but our connection was as such. She had a rawness that reminded me of my own mother and a countenance that reminded me of my aunt Rose.

SATURDAY JULY 13, 1991

My family and I were living on Lombard Street in Baltimore, Maryland. I don't remember the address, but I remember that street name because we crossed the street sign every day to go over to our babysitter's house. That special weekend, however, me and my brother were being watched by our Aunt Rose. She had the most beautiful round face that never had a scowl on it. She never lost her cool and she never acted out of anything but love. She carried around a thick long toothed comb that she used to brush down her silky graying hair. Every other woman I knew had curly, afro like hair or they permed it to make it straight. Aunt Rose's hair was long and wavy. Her hair flowed down to her lower back and my 4-year-old fingers loved running through it. Everyone has a family member that is the very definition of someone who loves Jesus. Aunt Rose was our definition. She took us to the grocery store with her to pick up a few things. While we were walking through the store, I got separated from her and Mark because I wasn't paying attention. I got distracted easily. I began wandering the store when I came across this toy troll on the ground. It was a brown troll with green hair. It looked interesting to me, so I picked it up. In my negligence, I didn't see or realize there was an entire stack of trolls on the cart beside me.

"Jay!" Mark screamed at me from the other side of the store. "We about to leave you!" He shocked me when he called me, so I jumped and ran towards him and Aunt Rose with the troll still in my hand. "Jay, take these bags, we gotta go." Aunt Rose handed me a few bags. On instinct, I put the troll in my pocket so I could get the bags. At that age, I didn't understand the concept of stealing. I just needed my hands to be free for the bags. We left the store and went home. As we were unloading the groceries, I pulled the troll out of my pocket. Mark's eyes welled up and in an inadvertent expression of shock he said, "oooooooooooo…" Aunt Rose turned towards us to see what the fuss was about, and she saw the troll in my hand. "Jay, where you get that from?" She inched towards me. "The store," I said proudly. I do not remember how Aunt Rose's face looked, but I could guess that she wasn't pleased. She took my hand with the troll in it and pulled me to her. With her other hand she grabbed her thick long toothed comb and began plunking it against my knuckles. With each hit, I felt a hot surge across my hand. I imagined fire floating above my knuckles, she was hitting it with such force. It was painful and I was crying, but not because it hurt. I'm not sure if I've ever cried from physical pain. I was crying because apparently, I had done something to disappoint Aunt Rose.

I must remind you that I was socially inept, especially at that age, so I had no idea what I had done. Customarily, amongst most or all black mothers, with each strike Aunt Rose revealed her reason for punishing me. "You will not steal another thing." Each word was a hit. I'm sure there were more words, but I understood the point, so I didn't keep record of it. I dropped the troll. I didn't even like toy trolls. If I was going to steal something on purpose, it was going to be Donatello from the Teenage Mutant Ninja Turtles.

PRESENT

I can see this being a point of trauma for most people, but for some reason I've always been able to see what others don't. Maybe I was given that gift to make up for my social deficiencies. What Aunt Rose did that day didn't teach me not to steal. That wasn't my problem. She taught me the skill and the importance of paying attention. I'm a slow learner, but once I get it, I never not get it again.

SATURDAY JULY 13, 1991

After my nap, because everyone takes a nap after a whooping, I sat on the floor pretending to play with my toys. I was watching Aunt Rose, and using my gift, I saw that it shredded her to have to discipline me the way that she did. It shredded her even more that she felt she had to. Our family history and the law has not always had the best relationship. I could see her praying while she was cooking my favorite food. She didn't want the same fate as some of my uncles to befall me. It's rather beautiful how our humanity could make us hopeful and worrisome at the same time. Seeing that battle in Aunt Rose while she was cooking showed me the tenderness of her love and the strength of her faith. That would be the first and only time Aunt Rose would discipline me.

WEDNESDAY APRIL 9, 2008

That's the person Tasha reminded me of. "I been around. I'm ok." I responded to Tasha. "How's the music going?" When Tasha asked me that, I felt embarrassed. I realized in that moment that a big part of me not coming to church had a lot to do with music.

3. TATTED UP

I was at the World-Famous Royal Peacock for an open mic competition called "ATL'S MOST WANTED TALENT SHOWCASE: BEST OF THE BEST." It was a collection of the best artists in the city competing for a cash prize and a spot on the radio. For those who don't know, the Royal Peacock was a historical monument in the black Atlanta community. Just a few names of people who have come through those doors and performed on that stage were Louis Armstrong, Ray Charles, Little Richard, and Marvin Gaye to Muhammad Ali and Martin Luther King Jr. We were performing on historical grounds, and we got to do it every week, if we were good enough. These were tough crowds. Even though the show didn't start until 9:30pm, artists would arrive as early as 2pm in order to get a spot on the stage. That's where I met some of the most talented independent artists of nearly every genre. Artists like Cotty, Willie Joe, Haziq Ali, Newz Huddle, BlackOut, All In Click, V.I.C., Marv And Cash and so many more. This is also the show that discovered and broke the artist Yung Joc with his song "Its Goin Down". The show was hosted by Akini The Black Mack of the A-Team morning show. The morning show was on Hot 107.9 with Griff, Rashan Ali, Emperer Searcy and Beyonce Alowishus. It was the most popular morning show until it was replaced by the Rickey Smiley morning show in 2008.

I had been performing at this showcase on and off since the summer of 2005. It was 2006 when I started to gain traction and quite the reputation as an exceptional lyricist and an electric performer. A manager and promoter friend of mine, Extra, would always tell me how I confused and surprised him at the same time. "It's like you the quietest person in the room. Then you get on stage and turn into the Incredible Hulk! Like Dr Jekyll and Mr Hyde." What Extra didn't know is that I was having a heart attack just at the thought of performing. My nervousness and my social anxiety would be bubbling inside of me like a volcano waiting to erupt. By the time I got on the stage, all of that nervous and pent-up energy would flood out of me uncontrollably. What I felt and what they saw were two completely different things. They saw me wrecking the stage, I felt like a nervous wreck. I was 19 years old surrounded by full grown adults and they're treating me as their peer based upon my talent. I guess it also helped that I looked 35. Although it nearly killed me each time I went on stage, my love for music and the arts was just a little stronger each time.

My name was called, "General Heat, come to the stage!" The volcano was simmering. Now, the normal greeting on a hip hop stage is one of loud and bold proclamations and instructions. "Get yo muthafuckin' hands up!" Or "Ladies, if you ugly, be quiet!" Or "We about to get live in this bitch!" As much as I love hip hop, those introductions weren't me and I was a terrible actor. So when I got on the stage I said, "What up y'all! Thank yall for coming out. Aight, DJ Brad, let's go!" If there's a life lesson I could give someone. It would be to remember people's names, even if they don't remember yours. That was important to me. That's important to people, whether they like to admit it or not. DJ Brad was the main DJ of the showcase. We may have had guests every now and then, but Brad was the guy. Gifted scratcher, keen ear for music and funny sense of humor who sometimes moonlighted as a party MC. He knew just what to say to raise the energy in the room. When he started the music, I transformed. I performed a song that had become quite popular in our showcase circle, "Put It In The Air". This was a phrase used for one to represent where they're from. I'm from

Baltimore, Maryland and there this phrase was primarily used for gang signs. In Atlanta, however, the phrase is used as a sign of respect and acknowledgement for where someone grew up. There were people from the Westside, Eastside, Southside and more recently the Northside. As I performed, the audience and artists began crowding the stage representing where they were from. It was a song that brought people together. Of course, I didn't know. I was 17 when I wrote the song. I just wanted to create something that excited people as much as it excited me. The song ended and I received a standing ovation.

On that night, I came the closest to winning the competition, taking 2nd place. 1st place went to the talented V.I.C. Whenever you're at a wedding or a family function or any kind of party, I'm pretty sure you'll hear the song "WOBBLE". Well while you're showing your best line dance moves, just know that song came from V.I.C. He was a phenomenal wordsmith, but by speaking to him he also knew the entertainment business well enough to know what people wanted to hear. That made him brilliant, and it was something that I would find myself struggling with for the next decade. The night wasn't a complete loss though. After congratulating V.I.C. I was then congratulated by hip hop duo Da BackWudz and the rap legend MC Shan. I made an impression on them, so they greeted me with kind words and told me to keep going. MC Shan even invited me to his house to make music with him. It was a whirlwind for me because these were the guys I'd been seeing on TV watching their music videos. If that wasn't enough, after I finished speaking with MC Shan, I was tugged on the shoulder. It was friend and artist P.O.P. I was surprised to see him because he had been gone the past month. We usually saw each other every week at the showcase. "Hey, somebody wanna meet you." He spoke, pulling me towards him. Walking towards the bar, I saw butter Timberland boots, baggy blue jeans and a tight white t-shirt covering what looked like the physique of a professional wrestler. The guy looked like he just left the set of DMX "Ruff Ryder Anthem" video shoot. "Heat, this is Q. I been recording wit Q the past month." I shook his hand and looked him in the eye just like my daddy taught me. My hands were large, but his smothered mine. It felt like I was squeezing tree bark. "Heat! You look good out there tonight." He spoke as if he already knew me. P.O.P. and BlackOut had been talking about me during their studio sessions. "I want you to come record with us," Q spoke in my ear trying to over talk the music. "Come check us out tomorrow. If you like it, we can do some work together." I had been promised things before, so what struck me about this conversation was Q promised me nothing. He just extended an invitation. Before he even finished his sentence, I was already there.

Now there were artist showcases on every day of the week in Atlanta. Looking back, it was no coincidence that I chose Wednesdays, the same day as Bible study at the church we were attending, to participate in showcases. I also scheduled studio sessions for Sunday mornings. I remember saying before that I became apathetic towards church, that I wasn't angry, and I wasn't hurt. I think I lied. I was hurt and angry.

FALL 2005

I was 18 years old, and I felt great about everything. I had just finished my first semester in college. I had a really good job as a contractor's assistant, and I was working in the theater department at my school for work study. I just finished my first mixtape. I picked up a side gig editing books and I had this new amazing relationship with God. I just got saved. That's church slang for confessing with your mouth and believing in your heart that Jesus was born of a virgin, died for our sins and rose again for us to have eternal life and a relationship with God. Life was great and I was really close to going back to church service on a regular basis. My brother had just become the youth pastor earlier that year so I would sit in on his Bible studies and his youth services when I wasn't performing or working. He had this way of galvanizing people to a central cause and convincing them to stay the course. Even though he was the youth pastor, when I looked around, I sometimes saw more adults in his classes than kids. And there were a lot of kids. Mark, my brother, had always been popular when we were kids, but this was different. He was gravity and everyone was pulled towards him as a law of nature, it seemed. That would end up causing problems of its own but that also isn't my story to tell.

When he became youth pastor, he was 19 years old. He became a youth leader much earlier at 17 and a minister at 14. His age was kept secret for a few years at the church because leadership was afraid the youth wouldn't respect someone they saw as a peer in age. He would become too familiar. I thought that was stupid, but I kept my mouth shut. I'd known how old he was all my life and I still regarded him as a father figure. No one was more familiar than me. Anything he'd ask I'd do it. Which is funny because as kids I rebelled against everything he said. I trusted him. I had confidence in him. And I'd be a pit bull for him. That remains.

As the school year was ramping up, I had huge plans for the future. My producer, Kenneth Paryo, and I were going to be working on more music and promoting our mixtape. I really didn't put much effort into school, but I was doing well enough. I didn't want to be there, but I didn't mind if my being there satisfied the people I cared about the most. I gave my parents and brother hell when I dropped out of high school. I figured I owed them this much.

PRESENT

I want to give a brief intermission to acknowledge that what I'm about to write, I didn't realize until I began writing how much these next events affected me. Here we go.

FALL 2005

My brother and the youth went to a conference. When they came back, the next few weeks, all I heard about was the title, "The Truth Behind Hip Hop". There was a pastor gaining traction in the southeast with his teaching and DVD series "The Truth Behind Hip Hop". G. Craige Lewis, a pastor out of North Richland Hills, Texas believed that the culture and the music of hip hop was not only corrupt, but demonic. The consensus was that all hip-hop music was evil and worshiping the devil. I had countless people coming to me telling me that I was going to hell because my rapping was evil. The message of the conference took hold of almost everyone who went. Kids were taking their CDs and hip hop merchandise and destroying them at the church's altar. There was an all-out assault on rap, hip hop and the people who supported it. That included me. The youth was on board. The church was on board. And most devastatingly, my brother was on board.

At the time, no one on this planet could affect me emotionally. No one, except my brother, and now he was in full support of something that went completely against what I believed I was born to do. I knew my relationship with God was new but why would He tell me to do something that was evil in His eyes? It didn't help that most people began to treat me differently, as if I was their enemy combatant. I learned a monumental lesson during that time. When people are against an idea, they are also against the people they perceive to represent that idea as well. Human beings seem to have an inability to separate sin from sinner unless that sinner is them. I was furious. I was frustrated. I was hurt. I was confused. I was no longer confident in my gift, and I would not get that confidence back until nearly a decade later. A running thought that had taken residence in my brain since then was, "I must not be reading the same Bible as everyone else."

Are there parts of hip hop that's demonic? Absolutely. I'd come to find out that there are parts of the church that's demonic as well. Yet, I didn't see anyone destroying Bibles to purge that evil out. And you, reading this; there are also parts of you that are demonic. There are parts of me that are demonic. There are parts of all of us that are inspired by evil due to our disobedience to God. The objective is to confront that evil, not destroy the whole person. Unfortunately, that's a principle we haven't learned just yet. I learned why people not only leave church, but also abandon their faith. I was told that these teachings were from Jesus, but all I saw from the people who were listening to these teachings was judgment. These people didn't love me. They didn't know how. I couldn't judge them for that, but I could leave to spare myself more pain.

SEPTEMBER 2006

I had been recording at Q's studio for the last 3 months. Me, P.O.P., BlackOut, Skinny, Ty Cutta and sometimes CovaGirl. We recorded day and night. More like night for me. I was still in school during the day along with two jobs. One day while I was in class, P.O.P. stumbled across an instrumental to which he wrote and sang a catchy chorus to. Later, Skinny would write two rap verses. Q was impressed. As impressed as he was, he felt like the song needed an extra flare, so he called the manager of current popular artist, Fabo of D4L. That night it was just me, Q and Scott, our engineer, in the studio. They played the song for me before Fabo got there. It was already a hit to me.

"Tell me again, why you don't cuss in ya lyrics, Heat." Q turned towards me. "I wanted you on this one, but I need some 'bitches' and 'hoes' for this song." I smiled.

PRESENT

For those who don't know me well, profanity is my native language. That's not a joke nor is it hyperbole. I knew how to say the word, 'fuck' before I knew how to multiply. That's true for anyone who grew up in an inner city. Profanity is used to describe love, hate, happiness, sadness, excitement, pleasure and pain. I'll never judge someone who seems to curse too much because I know where that comes from, and I know the work it takes to subvert it. I'm still doing it. I spent years learning the English language and made it a point of conviction not to use profanity in my music as a practice. So far so good but I'm bound to slip one day.

SEPTEMBER 2006

That was a conviction that Q saw to be an inconvenience. He loved my talent, my skill, even my convictions, but he never lost sight that this conviction of mine would cost him money as our manager and label head. Hip hop didn't fare well with clean artists. The only multiple platinum clean artist we could ever think of was Will Smith and it had nearly been 10 years since he'd done so. There was always a stereotype that clean artists in hip hop were soft. I didn't care, though. I'm from Baltimore, I'm tired of being tough or hard. I worked hard to be soft, and I was enjoying the person I was turning into because of it. I've always wanted the things I create to produce life, not the opposite. I'm not entirely certain that all profanity is negative, but I know that if I'm going to use it in a song, it had to be intentional. My lyrics meant everything to me, so I didn't believe in word fillers. That would be a conviction I couldn't let go and it would end up costing me more than I was ready to give up.

Fabo, his manager and two other guys showed up to the studio. I became invisible again and I watched. Upon entering, Fabo was already a ball of energy. He spoke to everyone and lit the entire room up. The way people hear him on the song is the way he walked into the door. Fabo was having quite the run at the time. He was just coming off of a triple platinum single, "Laffy Taffy" and a certified gold album with his group. D4L created the dance craze of snap music that was sweeping the country in the 2000s. Everyone wanted to work with them, collectively and individually. Although they were a group, Fabo seemed to be the face people saw the most. Q explained the song to Fabo. Fabo nodded his head in affirmation of what Q was saying. He asked to hear the song again and about 45 seconds into it he was ready to go. The most fascinating thing happened. He walked into the booth and the two guys who were with him, followed him into the booth. During the recording, the two guys were doing ad libs while Fabo was recording his verse. I had never seen that before. I'd never seen an artist have someone do their ad libs while they were recording. Full disclosure, the entire session may have taken 5 or 6 takes. That was inclusive of verse ad libs and background vocals. Fabo was lit but he was also a consummate professional. Once he finished his part, the song was finished. The song was called "Tattoo" but everyone referred to it as "Tatted Up".

By the standards, guidelines and culture of where hip hop was at the time, this was a guaranteed hit, and it was time to start performing. Q was making plans for a promotional tour and strategizing the best marketing schemes. He was ready to put this song everywhere. A few days later, I was in school when I got a call from BlackOut telling me that P.O.P. was arrested and he'd be in there a while. That was the voice of the chorus we were talking about. When we all got to the studio, Q was unphased. He just said the performances would have to be a collective effort on our part. That meant me, Ty Cutta and BlackOut, who were not on the song, would perform the chorus in concert. Q wouldn't be moved, and we stayed the course. A little under a week later, we'd be shaken again. I received another phone call while I was in school. This time it was from Q. He wanted me to come by the studio after class.

As I was making my way downstairs to the studio, I could hear the Tatted Up song playing with very distinct differences in the voices. Walking in, I saw Scott at the engineering desk and Q standing behind him. I greeted both of them, but I also heard an unfamiliar voice coming from the booth. "Stop the song, Scott. Aye, G! Come out here real quick." Q bellowed even though there was a talk back microphone at Scott's desk. Bursting out of the door was a small framed, fair skinned, colorful clothes wearing guy with a look on his face that screamed, "I'm happy to be here." "Face G, this is Heat, another one of my artists. Face G is gonna be doing the verses to Tatted Up since Skinny got locked up yesterday." Words were falling out of Q's mouth, but I don't think I heard him correctly. I nodded at him, shook Face G hand, eye contact, and I sat down so I could process. "Heat, I just want you to tell me how these verses sound and if they are good enough."

"Wait, wait, wait!" My brain screamed. I'm trying to process what's going on and Q just keeps talking. Let's see if I got this right. "Skinny is locked up; but for what? Nevermind, one thing at a time. This Face G guy is here to write and record new verses for the song; but where did he come from? Why didn't Q have BlackOut or CovaGirl do it? Stop, too many questions, James. Focus on what's in front of you. Now I'm here to make sure his verses are good? I mean, I'm always down to work as a team, but am I betraying Skinny just by being here? He's being taken off the biggest song of his career and in a way, I'm helping that happen. Well, he is locked up. Does that even make a difference, though? Can't we wait for him to get out? Well, how long will it be before he gets out? I don't even know what he's in there for. Let me listen to what this Face G guy got." That's my brain processing as Face G is walking back into the booth.

"Yeah, Skinny got his dumb ass locked up. Almost ruined the whole song. I met G at a showcase, and he got a similar style as Skinny." Q continued to speak. "Why can't these lil' niggas have they head on straight like you, Heat?" My brain was far too overwhelmed with new information to be answering questions or responding to flattery. Q and I had an interesting relationship. We had philosophical similarities on just about everything except for my convictions on my music and how to treat people in business. Oh yeah, and women. We had staggering differences on how to treat women. "I can tell you come from a two-parent household," he never stopped talking. That was ok for me because I never stopped listening. "Stop right quick, Scott." I cut Q's last sentence off because I heard something in Face G's verse that could use adjusting. It wasn't anything major, but because of my insane attention to detail I pointed it out. He ended up doing the same thing over again, so I let it go. I was still half listening to the song and half listening to Q vent his frustrations with the members of our group.

A few hours passed and the song was complete, again. We all agreed that this was it. We recorded a couple more songs before we called it a night. It was close to 2am when all was finished, and I was tasked with driving Scott home. I was often the one to take Scott home after our sessions because I was usually the last to leave. Scott and I would always have deep and meaningful conversations on our ride to his house. I noticed that he would light up differently when it was my turn to record a song. He was always interested in what I had to say. Every artist in our group never lacked talent, yet we were all different. I believe that's why Q brought us together. I had recorded a song about having a woman who would be always by your side no matter the situation. It was the last song of the night and Q didn't like it. "Heat, I like the song, but that's not gonna bring the bitches to you. And the bitches buy the records. Think about it like this; this song is for one woman. I need you to make songs for all women." Again, with me processing, I didn't respond right away. I saw his point; I just didn't agree with it.

"Heat, I'm all for having a woman you love and deeming her as the only one you're going to have sex with," Scott spoke as we drove to his house. "It may not be what Q or the others are looking for, but someone is looking for that." Scott gave me the reassurance that I needed; an assurance that let me know I was headed in the right direction. It was interesting, Q would always affirm my humanity, but I would always get the feeling that he didn't want my humanity in my music. This started to feel a lot like church. They want the parts of you that benefit them while also being unwilling to accept the parts of you that don't. "You know what, Heat? I don't know how long you're gonna be a rapper, I mean I hope you don't stop. But every time I hear you, I see you being a professor. You're always teaching." I was floored. I was recording the same music in the studio, and these two people have two completely different views of me when they listened. It's possible that that's because Scott and Q have two different and sometimes opposing objectives. It was Q's objective to make hit records for the public according to their taste. It was Scott's objective to make the best record sonically according to his taste.

About a few weeks later I got another phone call from BlackOut telling me that Skinny was back home and to come by the studio. "Uh oh," I thought to myself. I was headed to the studio to confess to Skinny that I was there when he was taken off the song and to possibly smooth things over with him and Face G in case there was any friction. To my surprise, while I was walking down the stairs to enter the studio, I heard Tatted Up with distinct differences again. I walked in and almost everyone is there. BlackOut, Ty Cutta, Q, Scott, even members of our promo team were there. There was no CovaGirl, we hadn't seen her in a while. No P.O.P., he was still locked up. And surprisingly, No Face G. I greeted everyone while keeping my ears open to the music that was playing. I heard Face G's lyrics to Tatted Up, but I also heard a different voice. The booth door opened, and it was Skinny. Apparently, Q had Skinny re-record Face G's verses to the song. I looked around and noticed that no one currently in the room was there when Face G first recorded his verses, no one but me Q and Scott. I looked at Q and he was bouncing to the music. I looked at Scott and everything on his face said, "none of my business." Great, just great. More for me to process, so I sat down directly behind Scott. I didn't know who knew what but judging from the look on Scott's face, I don't think it mattered. I had this eerie feeling that this was normal in our industry.

People started trickling out hours later and again it was just me, Q and Scott. "James, shut up. Don't ask nothin! But I need to know. No, you don't. You will not be able to unhear the answer. I still need to know." That was my brain. "Q, what happened with Face G?" I asked as Scott was packing his stuff up. "Damn it, James! You just couldn't help yourself, could you?" Sometimes, my brain doesn't agree with me. "He didn't wanna sign the contract I had for him. So I said, 'fuck him'. This my studio, my money, my masters. His verses was better than Skinny's but Skinny sounds better on his verses." I was right. I would never be able to unhear what I just heard. I didn't know Face G well but I remember his excitement and his confidence and even deeper, his hopefulness. "Wait, you gave him a contract to sign? Why didn't any of us get a contract? If we do get a contract and we don't like it, are you going to treat us the same way? Wait, Face G's lyrics didn't belong to him?" Boy did I have questions, but I didn't have a voice. My 19-year-old self only had a brain.

Tatted Up featuring Fabo was complete. Next, we perform. Q brought in a friend of his and fellow artist, Citty

Da Cookie Man. I was a fan of Citty and his work ethic. In the year 2005, Citty had done 330 shows in one calendar year. He was there to help us with our stage show and to give us credibility during performances. Yes, we had Fabo on the song, but he was far too busy to be at every show with us. We needed someone recognizable in the spaces we were going. Why not the man who performed everywhere the previous year? We were set, me, Ty, Black, Skinny and Citty. Each week, we may have done at least 3 to 5 shows. There was not one stage in the Atlanta metropolitan area that we did not touch. I loved the energy of the performances, but that's about it. I was never a big club goer. It didn't excite me. I'd usually stay to myself until it was time for us to perform. I didn't drink while we were out. I didn't eat until we were finished, and I didn't participate in the extracurricular activities after the shows. I never judged it; it just wasn't my speed. Everyone in the group respected that, but it became a point of hostility for Q towards me. I didn't know until much later that Q thought that as we got bigger and more popular, my convictions would change. It was a game for him to see how long it would take for me to break. When I wouldn't, I was no longer an asset to him, and the game was no longer amusing. As much as he complained to me about the mindsets of our group members, he benefited from them, and I could see he was working hard to keep them in the same mind frame. It made him more money for our group members to be desperate, desolate and in need of him.

One of our biggest shows came in November. Magic City was not only a staple in the Atlanta community. It was also the place where most records got their first big break. Prior to that, we had performed at nearly every strip club in Atlanta. Q would give us all money to throw in the crowd and at the strippers. Every time, I would give my money to someone on our promo team. That infuriated Q. He respected me personally, but professionally I was an obstacle for him. Once we hit the stage at Magic City, it was the same drill. Everyone was given $1000 in dollar bills to throw out and I gave mine to the promo team to do it. They had fun with it, and they were way more engaging with the crowd. In my mind, I was there for work. My job was to perform. That's what I'd do. The performance went great, and it was that show that would elevate the song into superstardom. During that time in our culture, there were four songs playing nonstop in every club. There was "We Fly High" by Jim Jones, "Throw Some D's" by Rich Boy, "Party Like A RockStar" by The Shop Boyz and "Tatted Up" by us.

We began headlining and co-headlining shows in the outer cities around Atlanta. That was inclusive of Augusta, Macon, Columbus, Savannah and Athens. We made our way down to Tifton, GA for the Tifton vs Lowndes high school football game. We had Tatted Up t-shirts on and we were signing autographs the entire game. That was so odd to me. I never signed an autograph before, and I kept wondering how they knew who we were. The home team, Tifton ended up winning 13-3 so we left to prepare for our show not too far from the stadium. The show, same as any, was a success but instead of me going straight home I would have to go to the hotel. I was four hours away from home and I liked being home. Q got us two hotel rooms for the night. One for him and one for the group. Like any other show, the guys wanted to celebrate with some company for the night. I was alright with that, but, again, not my style. They respected that. BlackOut even offered to help get me my own room for the night. I told him I was ok. I'm a frugal spender. "I'll just chill in the car," I told him. "Go have a good time, man. I'm good."

In all honesty, I was more than ok. I was around people the entire day. I needed the alone time. I wrote, I meditated, I prayed, I listened to music. I then had a thought. "Q knew what he was doing," I thought to myself. 4 guys to 1 hotel room, after the show we just had? Women were already in the lobby before we even got to the hotel. He had been trying to do everything in his power to break my convictions and I never understood why until that night. The more I spent time with everyone, the more I became that teacher Scott was talking about. With each interaction, Q ran the risk of everyone respecting me more than him. The only thing that separated him from everyone else was money. He had more of it and most people wanted it. I was separated by my ideals and the fact that I never judged anyone with them. That was a fleeting thought because of course I capped it off with, "maybe it's just me. Maybe I'm trippin'."

4. STEAL KILL
DESTROY

DECEMBER 17, 2006

Q had been entertaining record label deals since late October. By then, we were something everyone wanted a piece of. Tatted Up was everywhere and we were all so close to 'reaping the rewards.' Those were Q's words. "Shut up, James. Don't say nothing." My brain was about to be reckless again. We were all in the studio that night discussing the future because it was coming fast. According to Q we had offers from Universal, Geffen and Asylum records for a label deal. That meant that these record labels would sign Q's record label, called NCE records (Nothing Comes Easy), and we would sign under Q. The offers were on the table. He just needed to decide which one to go with and who he was going to sign under him. He laid out everything he required of us in order to sign with him. From his perspective, he held all the cards because the song was the star, not us. He was explaining to us everything it took for us to get that far, more like everything he did for us to get that far. And then he said it again, "we so close to reaping the rewards." My brain couldn't help but respond, "reap who's rewards? Face G's for writing those verses? P.O.P. for singing a chorus he hadn't gotten to perform yet? Citty for putting us on the right stages? Or Fabo for making the song what it was? Shut up, James, not now."

Q, then, came to each of us individually and listed out all he required from us going forward. He went to BlackOut, Skinny, Ty Cutta and then he came to me. "Heat, I'm gonna take the General off your name. Just Heat, sounds better. And I want you to be more of like a Mase/Fabolous rapper. Speak to the bitches more. So, you gonna have to start cussin' in ya raps. I don't wanna hear no arguing on that shit. It's gotta be that way or it won't work for you." For all the times I had to sit and wait for my brain to process, that time I didn't. It was like I knew it was coming.

WEDNESDAY APRIL 23, 2003

A week after our first step show, we were all still on cloud 9. We accomplished something hard together and showed how tough we could be. The practices were hard. The routines were hard. The discipline was hard. And we not only survived, we flourished. I was going to church and Bible study every week and we had step practice every Wednesday before Bible study. We conditioned, practiced our routines and conditioned some more. We then would go to Bible study super sweaty. Well, the guys would. We didn't care. We went into the main Sanctuary for praise and worship. That's the part of church service where the music goes. Then we broke out into our classes. Me, Paul, Marcus, Terrence, Shamir and Chris made our way to the youth Sanctuary for high school class. We usually sat next to each other, passing battle raps to one another during class to pass the time. That week, however, we had a guest speaker. It was my brother, minister Marquis Boone. When he was introduced, Chris screamed out, "how he gonna teach us? He look younger than me!" Mark, my brother, responded, "Chris, shut up before I pull the rest of your buck teeth forward. I got a haystack waiting on you!" Everyone cracked up laughing, even Chris. As I stated before, people gravitated toward my brother.

He began teaching and no battle rap notes were being passed. We were engaged. We also didn't want to be caught passing notes for my brother to crack a joke on us. He had just turned 18 but no one knew except me and the other leaders. He was teaching us the pattern of the enemy.

Just about everyone in the class besides me was familiar with the phrase "steal, kill and destroy". He was breaking it down for us and he explained something that I wouldn't understand or encounter until years later. He told us that a way you can tell that the enemy is after you is when he tries to take your name and make it whatever he wants it to be. That is why you never allow someone to call you out of your name. In your name is your authority. Your authority is not in your title or your stature or your rank. Your authority is in your name. If you allow him to take that away from you, it'll be easier for him to kill and destroy you. He said another way to tell the enemy is after you is when he tries to change your identity. Our identity is our lifeline. It's our personalities, our desires, our convictions and our relationship with God. If you allow him to change your identity, it'll be easier for him to destroy you. He then said a way to tell the enemy is after us is he tries to put us in a position where we can't say no to him. The enemy will try to strip everything away from you so that your only lifeline is him. As a 16-year-old, I never forgot that lesson.

DECEMBER 17, 2006

"No," I said. "I can't do that." In the time we've known each other, Q had never yelled in anger or lost his cool with me. That was about to change. He lost it, "Yes, the fuck you can! If you wanna make this money, you can. I'm sick of every show, you just standing in the corner with ya bottom lip in ya mouth away from everybody. And you giving ya strip club money to Jay Rock. Your music not good enough to do what you tryin' to do. You got nice verses and no hooks. I can help you with your hooks, but I'm not writing no fuckin' hook about corny shit like inspiration or being a good person. We need club bangers and you ain't got none!" I let him speak. It sounded as if these were the things he had been waiting to say to me for a long time so I let him get it all out. "Eye contact, James," I thought to myself. I watched him as he continued his tirade. The rest of the group watched in shock. They had never seen Q talk to me that way either. According to them, I was probably his favorite. I knew Q liked and admired me as a person, but that wasn't good enough to quell the greed that he called his business mind. I didn't judge him nor hate him for that. Instead, once he finished, I stood up, grabbed my bookbag and said to him, "no." I walked out the door. That would be the last time I'd step foot in his studio.

I didn't want to leave. I wanted to stay. I wanted to find common ground. I wanted to finish what we started, but I knew that would be impossible because for it to work out I would have to be the one to compromise completely. And the things he's requiring me to compromise are non-negotiable. I was angry. I was frustrated. I was hurt. Just a year ago, I faced the same rejection from church because they believed what I represented worshiped the devil. It was becoming clear to me that the church world and the non-church world didn't want me. Once again, I found myself not belonging anywhere.

BlackOut called me the next day and told me to just come by the studio, "we can fix this. We supposed to be gettin contracts next week for Christmas." For any artist anywhere, that's music to our ears. People spend their entire lives working toward a record deal. As a 20-year-old, three years after recording my first song, that dream could be a reality. At the time, I really saw it as a huge missed opportunity, an opportunity that I couldn't take advantage of if I wanted to. I called Q to apologize for the way I left, but he didn't answer. "Just come to the studio now. He here." BlackOut told me again. I wanted to, I really did, but I couldn't. It was over.

During the week of Christmas, daddy told me that I had mail. It was a brown clasp envelope. I opened it up and it was a contract agreement from NCE/Asylum Records. I read it. In the agreement, my name would be 'Heat' and my masters belonged to Q. It was a 3-album deal, which meant I'd be tethered to Q's newly constructed version of me. If

I'm being honest with myself, I didn't think I wanted anything that bad. I took the contract, put it back in the brown clasp envelope and placed it in the kitchen drawer.

WEDNESDAY APRIL 9, 2008

"Music is ok. I'm trying to figure some stuff out." I wouldn't lie to Tasha. I had no idea what I was supposed to do with music. I loved music because I loved poetry. I loved poetry because I loved words. I loved words because at an early age it was revealed to me that they were the most powerful things in the world, and it was something no one could ever stop learning. Yet with all of that love, I had no idea what to do with it. When I wanted to use my love of music, poetry and words at church, I was told I was going to hell. When I wanted to use my love of music, poetry and words in what church people call 'the world', I was told nobody wanted to hear what I had to say. The world didn't want me and neither did the church. As bad as that may sound, the worst part of it is that, at that point in my life, I accepted it.

I was tired of being beaten over the head with church tradition and having my legs cut from under me by a world telling me I was too positive. I was done… ish. I hadn't performed in over 8 months; I was so defeated. Even though I was crushed, I couldn't turn off my love for the music, the poetry, the words. So, I learned how to audio engineer recording sessions. I was taught by Michael Danners, who I had met a year prior and began recording with on a regular basis. I was a natural. I could hear things no one else was listening for and Mike helped me put what I heard into the music we made. He'd let me sit in on sessions he had with clients and even allowed me to engineer a few of them. Instead of introducing myself as a rapper or an artist, I would now introduce myself as an audio engineer. It was more respectable. Mike and I even started going into business together doing multimedia. I stayed as close as I could to music without being in the forefront and made money engineering while doing it. It felt like a pretty good consolation prize even though Mike would always remind me that my first choice was music, making it, creating it.

I was recording my own music in secret. No one else knew but Mike. No one else heard it but Mike, especially since the studio booth I was recording in was 7ft away from his bedroom. I had the courage to record what I was creating, but not enough to show the rest of the world.

PRESENT

There are still songs I recorded in that time period that have not seen the light of day. I guess some of that pain is still there.

JUNE 2007

Alongside my producer, Kenneth Paryo, I released a mixtape called "Prince Of The Flow". Housed in the mixtape was all of the pain, anger and rejection I felt from the past two years. Being told I was going to hell for being a rapper, rejected out of my group because of my convictions, even breaking up with my girlfriend; everything I felt went into the mixtape. It was massive to anyone who heard it. Filled with such skill, cultural ingenuity and a fire that reached a tipping point I didn't think was possible in my personality; I was getting a reputation as a force. I never said it aloud, but I wasn't happy with it. The mixtape was great, but it wasn't good. It was tough but without tact. It was a fire spread irresponsibly. Amongst the people who heard it, it was a hit, but it wasn't me. Nearly every song I visualized Q or someone from church repeating those words that cut slices of torment into my skin. I was trying to prove them wrong. What I ended up doing was digging myself deeper into a prison that I wasn't even aware I was in. Held captive by the words, thoughts and preferences of other people, I thought my only weapons for getting out of that prison were those same words, thoughts and preferences.

I was wrong about that, even though that process had been a practice many others have used toward their success. 'Use the haters as motivation' they say. 'Prove them wrong' they say. 'Use it as fuel for the fire' they say. What they don't tell you is that using the venom once used against you does provide an adrenaline boost that carries you through your current task, but it never sustains you for your major cause. My anger carried me through the mixtape, yet when that anger began to subside, I was embarrassed by my work. It was a great project to improve my skill, but I've always considered my words to be my greatest tools and I began using them as weapons the same way others did to me.

About two months later, I was outside of Club Crucial. It's a club belonging to the rapper, actor and activist, TI. On Mondays, they held showcases for up-and-coming artists, giving the winner an opportunity to open for TI or another major artist at a concert. While I was in line, I heard some commotion behind me. A few guys were laughing and joking using their outside voices. I'd come to know them as Sir Will and CP. When I turned around, I was greeted by the guy in front of them, "what's up, I'm Mic D." "General Heat," I replied. I recognized him from the Royal Peacock weeks before. He had been going around offering his graphics and production services while also performing. We spoke until we went inside, and he invited me to his studio to remix a song with him.

When I went to Mic D's studio, it took about 30 minutes for us to do the remix, but I was there for almost 6 hours. Yes, Mic D is the same Mike who taught me how to engineer audio. We spoke about everything from music to film to future plans. At the end of our session, as I was leaving, I gave Mike money for the studio session. He handed it back to me. "If you ever need anything, I got you.

Anything." I said that to him without hesitation. "Same here," he responded.

The next Sunday after my session with Mike, I went to church. My producer, Kenneth Paryo, played the piano for church. He was also a dancer. There was a special presentation he was involved in along with many other people I knew and loved, so I wanted to support them. Anchored by the musical genius of Korey Bowie, the presentation was mind boggling. It looked like there were 50 people on stage as they sang, danced and presented this piece of art they had been practicing and rehearsing for weeks. It was magical. It was intense. It was energetic. It was hip hop… My head tilted as I watched, and I sat down to think.

"Wait a minute… now this shit is ok?" I thought to myself. I looked back up at the stage to make sure no one was bursting into flames or spiraling down to hell. "Nope, everybody is still there." My thoughts began to run away from me. They were jumping, smiling so gleefully, dancing with such vigor and giving their complete all to their performances. I was happy for them, yet there was a large part of me that was confused, taken aback and angry. I had just spent the last two years of my life being told that the thing that I do and represent, hip hop, was causing me to go to hell because I was worshiping the devil. What. The. Fuck. I'm thinking I've reached my quota for cuss words. I didn't say anything because, of course, in my head I said, "Maybe it's me. Maybe I'm trippin'."

I won't lie. The back-and-forth interaction with me, church and hip hop put a barrier and a seed of contentious aggression in my relationship with God. I couldn't pray. I couldn't meditate. I no longer knew how or if the relationship was going to work. Hip hop was the thing that brought me to God. I wouldn't have been interested in any type of relationship with God had my brother not taken me to the church when Marcus, Chris and Terrence were practicing for their show. That was hip hop. Then, 2 years later, tell me that that interaction, in fact, was me worshiping the devil because hip hop is demonic. Just to show me, 2 years after that, that now hip hop is ok again. I was lost. I was conflicted. I was angry that I allowed these people I trusted to give me advice on something that, evidently, they weren't sure about themselves.

I listened to them tell me that I didn't need to be a rapper because that's not what God ordained. I listened to them when they told me it was sending me to hell. I listened to them when they told me I was demonic. I even listened and overheard my youth leaders talking amongst themselves about how stupid rappers are and how they don't need us to become them. "Why did I listen to these people about something they knew nothing about?" I had so many anger filled questions for myself because I didn't blame them for being ignorant. I blamed myself for listening and believing what they said for as long as I did. "How could I have been so stupid? Where in the Bible did it say I'd go to hell for rapping?" These were questions I was asking myself during the church service. An impressionable 18-year-old kid, with a brand-new relationship with God had his confidence, his inspiration and his belief in himself shredded because apparently God had some shitty misinformed representatives. After their performance, I stood, and I left.

5. SEMICOLON

TUESDAY SEPTEMBER 18, 2007

So, I was in the parking lot of Target after I just filled out a job application. I was jobless for a few months after losing both of my jobs over the summer. I had a little bit of money saved, but it was slowly running out. I needed something fast, or I was going to have to break down and tell my parents that I dropped out of college back in January. Mike, along with a few new friends I made over the summer all worked at Target and said they could get me in. I was grateful. Already overwhelmed by the misfortune I experienced the past year, I couldn't handle much more going wrong. In the last 10 months I've been broken up from my group, broken up from my girlfriend, dropped out of college, created a mixtape I wasn't proud of, lost both of my jobs and reminded why I stopped going to church. Now, I don't think the bad ever outweighs the good, the list of bad just happens to be longer. Getting the job would be a step in the right direction.

As I was walking to the car, I was unwrapping the plastic of an album I just bought. My former group's, The Alliance, album was released today, and I wanted to support my guys. Even though I had been out of the group for nearly a year, I was still in touch with the members of the group, especially BlackOut and Ty Cutta. On my way home as I was listening to the album, I came across track number nine. It was a song called 'Rub A Dub'. The song was an ode to the Caribbean heritage and their contribution to music worldwide, especially in the culture of hip hop. I was very familiar with the song because it was a song we recorded together in November of the previous year. Once I left the group, I was replaced by the rapper named Bliss. I didn't know anything about her, but I remember having a conversation with BlackOut months ago about her. He was telling me that Q was having her redo verses on songs that I was a part of. I didn't make anything of it at the time because I was dealing with my own stuff. What I failed to recognize was when BlackOut said the word 'redo', that meant my words were being taken and recited. A few things were changed to make the verse more gender specific for her, but those were my words.

A heavy cloud of fury covered me, and I could barely drive myself home. Listening to her use my words, my inflections, my cadences and my art broke something inside of me that was already fragile to begin with. Bliss was the voice I heard on the record, but I knew the instructions came from Q. I didn't know why I was so surprised, but it bewildered me to think that he could or would do that to me. I thought we were better than that. I also understood I was naive to think that. He was a man who engineered the theft of a hit song without blinking. I shouldn't have been surprised. I probably wasn't. I was probably using surprise to hide how hurt I was. I was devastated. Ignorant to copyright law, there was no way for me to combat something like that and I didn't have the energy for it. I didn't care about the money anyway. I cared that my art was stolen and made into a lesser version of itself. I cared that my friendship, kindness and consideration was taken advantage of. I was hurt because even though the success of the project twisted a knife inside of me, I still wanted it to succeed because that meant success for my former group mates.

It hurts to love those who spitefully use you. I knew that in my mind, but that hurt was too much for my 20-year-old heart to handle. For the last 8 or 9 months, I had been taking Nyquil in order to go to sleep at night. It started out as small doses. I used to explain it as I just couldn't sleep and the Nyquil would help me, but the reality was if I took enough of it, it would stop me from feeling everything that I was feeling. Pain, failure, betrayal, confusion, worry, doubt, and those were just the ones my grasp of the English language could name. Those small doses increased over time. The more Nyquil I took, the less effect it began to have on me. Before I knew it, I was going through boxes of it on a weekly basis. On that day, I took as much as I could without vomiting it up. I can't definitively say that I was trying to kill myself by overdosing, but I know I wasn't averse to it. I didn't care anymore, and I convinced myself that no one else would either.

The room got hazy as I was watching rerun episodes of The Fresh Prince on "Nick At Nite". Nickelodeon's nighttime programs would play old 90s sitcoms throughout the night on weekdays. It was the only thing I watched on TV at the time. It's been said that old TV shows sometimes serve as medicine to anxiety and depression by taking you back to a time of comfort, joy and happiness in your life. It could also be used as a coping mechanism. I made no arrangements. I didn't write a letter. I was never much of a planner. Those were my thoughts as I was dozing off. I wasn't thinking about all the things I'd been through the past year. I wasn't thinking about all the suffering I felt in silence. All I wanted was to sleep, forget and feel nothing. With a sort of eerie precision, I got what I wanted in a way I wouldn't dream of experiencing again.

My eyes opened to a dark room only lit by an episode of Roseanne playing on "Nick At Nite". I saw the show on the TV, but no sound was coming from it. I grabbed the remote to turn the volume up, still no sound. The volume bar had reached capacity before I began to panic. "My ears must be clogged. Am I going deaf?" My thoughts started to race away from me again. I jumped up to leave my room, but I couldn't get out. The door was locked. Each time I unlocked it, the doorknob still wouldn't budge. I was shaking the doorknob and started to panic again because I couldn't hear the door press against the door frame. I shook it harder, still no sound. I remember taking a few steps back while turning to the left toward my bed when I saw it. My mouth opened to scream, still no sound. I felt the pressure in my head from screaming so hard, but I couldn't feel any pain. I screamed so hard I felt beads of sweat dripping down my temples. I wiped my eyes and blinked aggressively as I stepped away from my bed. I couldn't believe what I was seeing. It was me, lying in my bed, motionless. "What is this? Is this what I look like when I die? Am I dead?" Even though those were my thoughts, and I knew I was thinking them, I still couldn't hear them. I inched toward my bed as slow as a snail to confirm that it was really me. It was. It was me, cold, dry, stiff. Nothing was moving on me except my chest. There were small pulses of my heart beating. It was slow, but it was there. I know that because it was the only thing I could feel. It was beating so hard that the vibrations traveled to my ears. I began looking around my room and knocking things over to see if I could hear or feel anything else. There was nothing, no sound. Yet when I looked over to my body on the bed, my heartbeats got louder.

In my room, I wrote scriptures on my walls from when I started my relationship with God at the age of 18. Psalms 51:1-2, Proverbs 3:5-6, James 1:12, 1 Peter 2:17, John 3:16 were all written directly on the walls of my bedroom, in pen. It never crossed my mind that maybe I shouldn't be writing on my wall, I just did it. Well, as I was inching toward my bed, viewing my body, those scriptures began to glow on my bedroom walls. With each scripture glowing, it revealed to me why each one was on my wall. John 3:16 to show the magnitude of how much God loves me. James 1:12 to show me the strength and endurance I have in myself. 1 Peter 2:17 to show me the honor and respect I use to treat others. Proverbs 3:5-6 to show me how to trust God when I don't understand. And Psalms 51:1-2 to show me God's patience, mercy and willingness to forgive no matter what I do.

Those glowing words began elevating off the wall and floating towards me, the me on the bed. Surging over my body, the glowing words were leaving particles of its light on my body, yet never taking away from its own glow. Abruptly, the glowing words stopped moving. It was almost as if the words recognized that all of me wasn't there and they stopped to look for me. My heart started beating faster. When it did, the glowing words found me, the standing me, and they flew towards me in great haste. There was a sense of urgency that startled me as the glowing words encircled me. I spun around trying to see what these glowing words were doing to me. As I was spinning and looking, I began to see that as the glowing words left pieces of its light on me it began to highlight other words, darker words.

Those dark words felt familiar, they felt native. I saw, 'you're going to hell' and 'that's demonic'. I also saw, 'you're not good enough' and 'you don't belong'. There were so many dark words and phrases being highlighted by the light the glowing words provided that I began to hear the voices that these dark words and phrases came from. The voices were loud and the louder they got, the glowing words that encircled me began to dim. My heartbeat started to slow. I continued looking around me and it looked like the glowing words of scripture and the dark words of negative origin were attacking each other. The dark words were so loud, I couldn't hear my heartbeat as clearly. With these glowing words dimming more and more, the dark words stopped. I stopped. The glowing words stopped. The dark words focused its attention on my body, my body on the bed still glowing from the light that the glowing words left on it.

The dark words rushed over to my body consuming all the light it had. My heartbeat got slower. The glowing words got dimmer. I felt myself getting weaker. Recognizing what was going on, I tried to scream, 'No!' There was no sound coming from me. All I could hear was the voices of the dark words and a fainting heartbeat that was being drowned out. I tried again and heard nothing, but I felt it. It felt like the pressure one feels sticking a q-tip in their ear. I tried again, pushing as hard as I could. I shouted, I bellowed, I screamed, and I sustained that scream. The harder I pushed, the pressure started to subside like a sonic wave reaching the end of a noise canceling tunnel. Harder, the veins in my neck began showing in more definition. Harder, I felt my eyes vibrating in its sockets. Harder, I felt the ramus of my jawbone cracking.

"NO!" I felt myself. I heard myself. I heard me over the voices of the dark words. My heartbeat got faster, the glowing words lit up again, the dark words began to scatter, and my room started to shake. I looked down and my floor was cracking apart. I ran towards my bed and jumped on it, right on top of me. The walls of my room were tumbling down and the ceiling was falling. I thought I was in a bad dream, so I pushed myself in the chest to wake me up. Nothing. I screamed, "wake up!" Nothing. I curled over my body to protect myself from the ceiling coming down. The room collapsed.

After a few moments, it got quiet. Everything stopped. I lifted my head to see myself still lying there motionless, cold, stiff and dry. I looked around and I saw nothing but water. The bed was floating over a body of water. I was terrified of being in large bodies of water. Yet, the water looked familiar; it smelled familiar. I felt like I'd been there before. As the bed was floating, I heard a voice screaming for help in the distance. I could hear again. The bed was floating towards the voice. The closer we got the more I could see that someone needed help. Someone was drowning in the middle of the water. The bed floated closer as if it was directed toward this person. I screamed, "Hey! Over here! I'm coming!" They couldn't hear me. The bed floated closer, close enough that I could get to the person drowning. "Turn around. Take my hand." I shouted for the person to hear me. They didn't hear me, but they turned around. It was me, the 14-year-old me, drowning. I reached my hand out to grab them, him, me. When I got close enough to touch him, he went under the water. Everything went black.

FRIDAY APRIL 06, 2001

Me and my family had been in Cape Hatteras, North Carolina on vacation for about a day. It was me, my brother, mommy, daddy, Aunt Berice, our cousin Auvea, aunt Berice boyfriend, I don't remember his name, and his son whose name I don't remember because he was named after his father. We decided to go Kayaking at the beach which was really the Atlantic Ocean. We're all having fun and we finished kayaking. The adults went back to the house we rented, with the exception of Aunt Berice's boyfriend. He stayed with us because we wanted to keep swimming. We all still had on our wetsuits from kayaking so there was no point in stopping. We got out there and we were swimming in the water. I decided that I wanted to go out a little farther than everyone else. I was warned that no lifeguards were on duty and no one I was with was a reliable swimmer at the time. I could swim, but I would later understand that you are not a reliable swimmer until you can swim under duress.

I went out farther anyway. I've always loved the water and I wanted to experience as much of it as I could. As I was swimming, the shore was getting smaller and I was beginning to no longer feel the sand under my feet. A few moments later something happened that I would later be told was called changing tides. That's where instead of the waves of the water pushing you back to shore, it would pull you out to sea. The tide changed and I got hit with a crashing wave that pulled me out to sea. I wasn't a great swimmer, but I was trying to get back to the shore the best way I knew how. Every time I felt one of my toes touching the sand, I got hit with another wave, pulling me out farther. After that cycle of events happened enough times, I got tired.

I was terrified because no matter how hard I paddled or how close I got to the shore, the waves just kept pulling me out to sea. I'm a fighter, but the ocean had much more stamina and endurance than I did. I was out there fighting and swimming for my life for what seemed to be a lifetime but would end up being clocked at about 15-20 minutes. I saw my brother running around on the beach trying to get someone to help, but I was being pulled out so far out that he kept getting smaller and smaller. I could see nothing but water. The shore was no longer in my eyesight, and I was exhausted. I began to picture myself dead in my casket, motionless, cold, stiff, dry. I pictured my own funeral because I didn't know if I was going to make it back. I was stranded. I thought I heard someone shouting from behind me, but I didn't have enough in me to turn around.

Those shouts sounded like they were getting closer and everything in me wanted to turn around. I heard the words, 'over here, I'm coming', but I was too focused on getting myself to the shore to respond. Then I heard the words, 'turn around, take my hand', as if someone was talking into my ear. I jerked my body to turn around and reached for a hand I thought I saw. Before I could see anything clearly, I got hit with another wave that pulled me under the water. I was under for a little while. I was so tired, I just wanted to rest, even though I knew I couldn't if I wanted to live. I gave all the energy I had to swim back up. When I did, there were 4 guys from New York on surfboards there to rescue me. They put me on a board and surfed me back to shore.

While we were surfing back, another wave hit us and threw me off the board. They pulled me up again and continued surfing me to safety. The entire time we were surfing back, I kept my eyes on my brother. He was on the sand praying. I'm pretty sure there were more people on the beach, but all I saw was him. As we got closer to shore, one of the surfers said to me, "make sure you kiss the ground once you get back". We reached the sand; I ran straight to my brother and hugged him. I, then, saw our little cousin Auvea and hugged her too. We walked back to the house. The next few weeks I was so terrified, I couldn't be around any water without feeling traumatized. I couldn't even take a shower without hyperventilating. I associated water with that experience so every time I saw water, I felt fear. During that time, however, my brother would remind me that it was God who saved my life.

THURSDAY SEPTEMBER 20, 2007

It was like I was watching the events of my life on TV. From the bed floating in the water, I could see myself drowning. I could see the 4 surfers from New York saving me. I watched them surf me to shore. I could even see myself hugging my brother once I got back. "How dare you try to take something that doesn't belong to you?" I heard it coming from the water. "How dare you try to take something We've worked so hard to keep alive?" I heard it again, and when I did the water began to shake. I heard thunder but there was no cloud in sight. There was no lightning. The shaking became more violent, and it tipped the bed over, tossing both me and my body into the water. Everything went dark again.

I couldn't see anything, but I could feel that I was back in my bedroom. The room was empty, no TV, no bed, nothing. I stood trying to regain my composure. There was nothing around me and then my walls began lighting up with the glowing words of scripture. The words encircled me again. This time, the dark words were gone. The glowing words floated in front of me forming a figure with light. The figure started to speak to me, I spoke back. That would be the first time I had an honest conversation and confrontation with God. The conversation was privileged, but I can say He wasn't too happy with my impulsive emotional decision to kill myself and our conversation would ensure that it would never happen again. Our conversation also taught me how to pray and how to meditate. He didn't just save my life; He saved my soul. Of course, the last thing I remember Him saying to me was, "Get up."

I woke up to an episode of The Fresh Prince on "Nick At Nite". I looked at my phone and it was 3:17am, Thursday morning. I had been out for over 28 hours. No wonder my bed was soaked in sweat and urine. Even though I was out for an entire day, I was exhausted. My body felt like it had been fighting for its life. I had this nasty medicine taste in my mouth that made me rush to the bathroom and vomit in the toilet. I took a shower, washed my sheets, thanked God and slept on the couch downstairs.

6. "HEAT, THE COMPUTER DIED."

I'm often asked how it is that nothing seems to bother me. I've never had an adequate answer before because I hadn't taken time to think about it. People around me tend to think that I'm bestowed this supernatural amount of patience, temperance and poise. I'm not sure how valid any of it is, but I am sure that I've been through enough to learn how to manage my information, my actions and my emotions. I don't believe in not taking things personally, I'm a person. I do believe, however, that learning how to manage the way we digest information prevents us from losing the power of our emotions by not succumbing to them. I also don't believe in controlling emotions.

I've done that before and that's not a sustainable resolution to protecting one's peace. When something happens to us and we have a natural internal reaction, our instinct is to control that emotion, to stop it from happening. "Don't let them see you sweat. Don't let them get to you." We've all been taught that. Well, we've been taught incorrectly. By doing this, we are smothering an emotion inside of us that needs a place to go and will come out one way or another. That emotion, that energy will, no doubt, come out as aggression, passive-aggression, resentment or even hatred the longer it's held onto. When we try to smother our emotions, we bury it in a volcano waiting to erupt at the most inopportune time. We think we are controlling something that isn't meant to be controlled.

Emotions are meant to be felt. Emotions are meant to be guided. Emotions are meant to be remembered. You don't get to control something that strikes at a moment's notice. A lot of us have trouble with our emotions because we've been trying to control them as if we own them. Controlling emotions is similar to controlling a teenager. You may think that you have them under control, but they're just waiting for the perfect time to show up and be themselves. And when they do show up to be themselves, we act surprised that it happened. Controlling our emotions also makes us look tough and poised to the outside world, while eating up everything inside of us. It's no wonder why we suffer from generations of stroke and heart disease.

Take anger, since that's the easiest example. We're taught and told not to be angry when something happens to us that produces anger inside of us. By doing that, we're swallowing that fever-pitched energy into this volcano of dormant emotion. After a while that fire goes down leading us to believe we have controlled that emotion, but the emotion is still there in our bodies biding its time. Think about it. What do your emotions want? They want to get out. They want to be free. Yet, we've been taught to keep them in and then wonder why so many of our people, young and old, have anger issues. It doesn't even matter what the emotion started out as. The longer we hold onto it, the higher chance it has of turning into anger.

I, personally, don't hug people when they're crying until they're finished. Who am I to get in the way of the physical manifestation of their cleansing? We've been taught to do that because it shows support. It shows that we care. I don't think either way is right or wrong, I'm just sharing what I've seen and experienced. Emotions aren't meant to be catered to irresponsibly, because emotions by themselves are manipulative. They seek to get out by any means and will jump onto another person in order to do so.

I have a process with my emotions that I practice. I feel them, I guide them, I remember them. It may sound elementary but feeling emotions is important. It's even more important to feel them completely. We have a habit of feeling our emotions until they get too uncomfortable or too intense. I make sure I feel everything, no matter how long that may take. If you're questioning how to feel it, I simply allow it by doing nothing. Our emotions have a way of traveling through our bodies with no help from us at all. The more you pay attention to it, the more you'll feel it. I tend to breathe intentionally through it. Once I do, instead of allowing it to sit and fester, I guide it out. I do this by applying stress to my body in the form of running, pushups, creating something, weightlifting or any other type of exercise, while focusing on guiding that emotion out of my body. The emotion is energy and although we don't get to control it, we are fully capable of transmuting it into something else. 'Transmute' means to change from one nature, substance, form, or condition into another. I transmute my emotion into breath. That's how I guide it out.

I did all of that explaining just to say that I manage my emotions by use of the Holy Spirit. The word 'spirit' is derived from the Latin word 'spiritus' which means 'breath'. When we panic, when we're angry, anxious, flustered or embarrassed, what do we forget to do? Breathe. We stop breathing. That's why our hearts start beating faster. That's why our vision gets blurry, and we see red. That's why beads of sweat begin forming when we're overcome with emotion. We don't breathe. American novelist Gregory Maguire once said, "Remember to breathe. It is, after all, the secret to life." One thing I know about secrets is that they're often filled with information everyone should know about. It's interesting and sometimes dumbfounding how the most powerful parts of us are as simple as something like breathing. Now consider that we are the only beings on the planet that God breathes into in order to have life.

After I feel my emotions, after I guide my emotions out of my body, I remember them. Some things are too painful for us to feel again so we'd rather just forget. I remember them as a part of my playbook. No, I'm not a glutton for punishment. Yet, we must understand that all emotion isn't negative and remembering the emotions I feel is used as information. The more information I have on my emotions, the better I can manage them. Good emotions must be managed too, or else they'll form into addictions. I also remember my emotions in order to practice how I manage them. Here's how powerful our brains are. Our brains don't tell the difference between actual and imagined danger. So, if I think or remember a time where my arm was broken, then my body will respond as if my arm is being broken. Thus, my body, my arm will feel the pain of it being broken. This is the same energy used when one has a panic or anxiety attack. In my meditation time, that's the energy I use to practice managing my emotions. This is the practice I use to increase my patience, temperance and poise. So yes, things do bother me, but I'm spending time in practice so that I can confront what I'm feeling faster and more effectively. I say this because things were not always this way.

MONDAY MAY 5, 2008

It had been a few months since Mike and I decided to do business together. After he taught me how to engineer sound last year, I got unusually good at it. He'd have me take the same song and mix it repeatedly from scratch to ensure I'd be good. Mike also did graphics, video and CD duplication. It was a one stop shop. Everything you needed in the media field, we had it covered. We were doing well for ourselves, so well that we quit our jobs at Target. It had been about 3 or 4 months since we quit, and we had some big projects in our queue. We had music projects, graphics projects and possible investors we were getting prepared for. The investors would be vital to us getting the equipment we needed to sustain ourselves. And since we both made music, we were focusing on that too. Over the weekend, Mike had produced, written and recorded a song that we could only describe as 'the best song ever'. Neither one of us could tell you the melody, cadence or genre of the song. We just knew that it was the best thing ever created. I went home that Sunday as Mike was still working on the song. Everyone was excited about it.

The next day, I was sitting in the living room, where I had been sleeping since September of the previous year, when I got a call from Mike. I thought he was calling me to see what I'd be doing for Cinco De Mayo. "What's up, you arduous, ancient asshole!" As a running joke, Mike and I would always greet each other with obscenities using alliteration to see who could come up with the best phrase. That day, there was no comeback. I was confused. There was a pause on the phone and then Mike would say something that I'd never forget. "Heat, the computer died." The computer that had all our projects on it, all of our videos on it, all of our music on it was gone. The most heartbreaking part of it was that with the money coming in from the investors, we were going to get a new hard drive. Everything we had been working on was gone. Deposit money for current projects had to be refunded because they couldn't be completed. Investor money would have to be used for repairs instead of expansion. And 'the best song ever' would have to be redone from scratch. The problem was, after being under so much stress from the computer, no one could remember what it sounded like. Slamming the phone down after I hung up, I began to ask God what I did that was so wrong. Like seriously, how many kicks in the ass do I really need?

After a few days of getting quotes and trying to find out if anything was salvageable, we began to accept that what we had was gone. Starting over was no longer just a possibility, it was our reality. We had a ritual. When we were celebrating something, even if it was just us getting paid, we would go to Ryan's Buffet to eat. When we were lamenting something or licking our wounds, we'd go to Burger King or Wendy's. We never set it up like that, it just seemed to happen that way. Well, we were headed to Burger King. Me, Mike and CP were about halfway to Burger King when mommy called me to tell me that she cooked. We all looked at each other, sitting in Cp's BMW, "home cooked meal or Burger King?" I asked rhetorically. "HOME COOKED MEAL!" We all shouted in unison. My parents loved Mike, Cp and the whole crew. They would randomly bring us stuff to the studio anytime I'd be gone for days or weeks at a time. They'd bring food, random gifts, they even bought a poker table for the studio.

Once we got to my parents' house, we ate, laughed and listened to music. That was daddy's specialty. Not ever knowing what's wrong, he just knew how to lift people's spirits. In an unrelated conversation, out of nowhere, daddy looks at Mike and says, "you like a jack of all trades, master of none. You are good at just about everything." I didn't think anything of it, since he uses that line on me, Mark and mommy so often, but it struck Mike differently. Not in an offensive way. Instead, Mike looked enlightened. It was almost as if a light bulb went off in his head. I just kept eating and chucked it up to something daddy always says. After all, I was thinking about how I was going to make money now.

Weeks later we were all feeling the effects of our national recession. Gas prices had risen to over $3 a gallon, jobs were sparse and just about everything was difficult. Even though Barack Obama was spreading hope with his 'yes we can' campaign, my household was having two cars being repossessed. I didn't even have enough gas to get to the studio. My emotions were everywhere. I couldn't rest. I couldn't eat. Sometimes I couldn't even think. I promised God that I wouldn't go back to taking Nyquil again, but I was having a hard time making sense of my situation. I started trying to control my emotions again and it was leaving me constipated in my mind. I didn't want my emotions to overtake me, so I held it all in and it was just waiting to erupt.

After a while and a few odd jobs later, I was able to make my way back to the studio. Mike had produced a record for Cp called 'Red Light' that was getting a lot of attention. It was a hip hop dance record that had all the makings of a hit if it got the right promotions. A manager by the name of London came to the studio right before I arrived. He wanted to talk to Mike, Cp and Rok D, Mike's older brother, about being in a group together. They would call themselves, 'Kumbined'. I initially felt left out, thinking if I had only been around, I could have been a part of the group too. But seeing that I hadn't touched a microphone in months, there wasn't much I could offer. Still emotionally drained I had just been going through the motions of living, searching for something that would excite me. I thought it would be the studio, but after my visit, I was wrong to think some sort of external simulation would jolt me out of something that was happening inside of me.

When everyone left for the night, Mike and I were in the studio as he expressed his reluctance about the group. "The moment I feel like they not working as hard as me, Heat, I'm out." Mike had this unwavering focus that reminded me of my brother. It's so interesting how the same event could affect people in two completely different ways. After the computer died, I was shattered, but something clicked in Mike that anchored him, lock in step. Catching up on everything we missed the past month, Mike asked me something that made me shudder in self-discovery. "When's the last time you created something, Heat?" The rest of our conversation faded as I could think of nothing but his question. I'm not sure if I even answered it. I needed to get in my car and drive. In the car is where I prayed, meditated and sought God's voice. It took me 3 hours to get home that night. Gas was at its highest, I still had no job, no clients and I had no plan for the future. None of that was on my mind. All I could think of was figuring out the answer to Mike's question and why it struck me so hard.

As was my ritual, I listened to the first 6 songs on the 'Speak Those Things' album by Fred Hammond in silence, preparing for me and God's conversation. 27 minutes and 16 seconds later I turned the music off. Circling around i-285 I began talking to God for about 30 minutes straight. I wasn't used to doing that much talking without interruption. After my last sentence I realized that I was speaking so long because it had been months since I'd even spoken to Him. Sure, I'd talk to Him in passing but not an actual conversation. I rambled on and I hadn't yet asked God about what I intended our conversation to be about. I was just unloading. My mouth going dry was an indication that it was a good time for me to stop talking. Passing by route 400, my reprimand began. I don't know how anyone else hears God's voice, but I hear Him as a wiser, funnier, sometimes condescending version of my own voice beating on my eardrums with a reverberated whisper.

He asked me how long I would allow my emotions to be my master. He reminded me of how He saved me from myself last year while making another emotional decision. And He let me know that I didn't have an anchor. I was drifting whichever way I was pushed, the same way my emotions were, and nothing was keeping me grounded. I had no vision. God then asked me a question. "What do you want?" It made sense to me. I didn't want anything. Growing up, I never wanted anything. I was too scared to. Anytime, I ever asked for something, the answer was no or I was told why I shouldn't want it. So, I stopped asking and after a while, I stopped wanting. I desired nothing, not because I knew it would be provided, but because I was afraid that it wouldn't. I sunk everything so deep inside of me that I couldn't find it anymore. "I don't know what I want!" I screamed as I passed by the airport for the second time.

A man without purpose and direction is lost. I was lost. It's fascinating how one could be lost and not know it, but once I said it I saw what happened to me. I couldn't create anything because I had no purpose to. I made a mixtape that I was unhappy with because I had no direction and the last time I trusted my direction; I was kicked out of my group. The last time I trusted my purpose, I was told I was going to hell. Anytime I did what God wanted me to do, it felt like I was punished for it. Once I was hit enough times, I sunk into myself and laid dormant. Me not creating was me lying dormant again and as a creative if I'm not creating, I'm dying. "I want to create. I want to make music again." I got off i-285 at the Covington Highway exit and headed home.

7. AM I MY BROTHERS'
KEEPER?

Ever since my drive with God a few months ago, I had just enough information to keep going. My relationship with God was strengthening and I had a partial hold on what I'm on earth to do. All it took was a partial vision to excite me. Coming from someone with no vision to start, that was big to me. I wasn't going to hell for being a rapper. There was a place for me, even though there were still others that didn't believe so. I began making and creating the music that I wanted to, the music I heard in my head. I began writing freer than I ever had. I began to move with an objective. Around Christmas of the previous year, I started working at Macy's along with Mike and CP. It was a great job with benefits and plenty of room for promotion. My objective had nothing to do with that though. I was working at Macy's to get enough money to build my own studio. My parents had a guest room in the house that wasn't being used so that's where I would build it. Each month I would count my money to see how close I was to my goal. The closer I got, the more excited I became. I had never been so focused in my life. That may have been the first time I'd written out a plan and executed it.

During that time, I had been invited by the musical genius, Korey Bowie, to be on his upcoming project. I was also recording more and more music at Mike's studio after we got off work. Invitations were coming from just about everywhere, but one mattered to me more than anyone else's. My brother was preparing for a youth conference that he would call, "Access Granted". The idea was creative and the theme of correlating one's relationship with God as an access point was brilliant to me. During his preparation, he asked me to write and record the theme song for the conference. My mind was blown. He said he wanted me to perform the song every night of the conference to kick the night off, in the main Sanctuary. It's one thing to do a rap for the choir, or even to do a song in youth church, but a full-on rap song in the main Sanctuary, on stage, at the altar, in the pulpit? That is the place where the pastor was designated to preach the word. That was sacred ground. There's no way church leadership knows about this. They'd go crazy if they saw a child running across the stage let alone perform this devil worshiping hip hop. I must be dreaming. If rapping sends you to hell, the conference would be my burial ground and I couldn't wait.

During my car trips with God, as they occurred more often, He'd show me more of who I was to Him. My relationship with church was shotty at best, but my relationship with God felt like I had a new best friend. The clarity, the acceptance, the peace, the creativity, the love He showed me through me was astonishing. Each car ride would provide a deeper level that I was elated to experience. My car became sacred. My car became my Sanctuary. Kenneth produced an instrumental that I would use to write my song for the conference. Per the theme of it, I called the song "Access Granted". I wrote it immediately and began recording. Periodically, as I was going through different takes of the verses, Mike would walk by and yell, "sounding good, Heat!" Writing the song gave a bird's eye view of the events of my last 4 years and it made me realize that faith triumphs in trouble. I had been in trouble internally, but with every mishap and devastation, my faith increased dramatically, and I didn't know it. I may have known nothing about church, but I was well acquainted with faith. The scripture of the conference was Romans 5:1-4 and those words embodied all I went through the last half decade.

"Therefore, having been justified by faith, we have peace with God through our Lord Jesus Christ, through whom also we have access by faith into this grace in which we stand, and rejoice in hope of the glory of God. And not only that, but we also glory in tribulations, knowing that tribulation produces perseverance; and perseverance, character; and character, hope.
Romans 5:1-4 NKJV"

Even though I'm a bit of a renegade when it comes to conventional and traditional ideals, I've recognized the power in my words. I never took that for granted. What I did overlook, however, was a sudden change in direction from my brother. My brother always supported me, but at that time, not so much in public. He was a huge reputationist. I'm pretty sure I made that word up, but he cared an awful lot about his reputation. So, showing me support so publicly against the traditions that gave him his platform grabbed my attention. I didn't have the words to ask a direct question, so I just watched him closely, more closely than I usually would. That's saying a lot. Throughout the spring of 2009, he began to exhibit a characteristic that I had only seen from myself and daddy. That characteristic was called 'fuck it'. The characteristic produces itself as one begins to reject the ideals and concepts that once brought comfort and acceptance in order to seek out a newly formed paradigm as one evolves. The characteristic was all over him. It became obvious the first night of the conference. The DJ was playing music, lights strobed, bass shook the building, kids were racing through the doors and my brother was dancing. It wasn't a plain 2 step or a church shout. He was dancing. I hadn't seen him dance like that since he entered dance competitions back in middle school. I had no idea what was going on with him, but it made me happy. He came to me sweating through the towel across his shoulder, "you ready? You going up next."

I hadn't been on stage to perform my own songs in two years. Of course, I was ready! I nodded, yes. He jumped on the stage, the pulpit, as if he was about to perform a song himself. He began speaking, hyping the crowd up. He was gravity. He introduced me and everyone cheered. I had been practicing nonstop the past month so I could perform with my eyes closed and with very little mental effort. My words were coming out with ease. My movements were fluid. My syncopation was flawless. I was on autopilot. I looked out into the crowd. They were rocking and swaying, catching onto and singing the chorus. They were screaming, "Access Granted." Looking into the crowd, my heart lit up. I began seeing faces that used to torment me. I saw kids, youth leaders and adults that were a part of the 'you going to hell because you rap' crew from years before. They were dancing the hardest, singing the loudest. Instead of seeking vengeance or some sort of recompense for how they treated me before, I felt compassion. I didn't feel like I needed to get back at them or show them how wrong they were. I felt the need to embrace them and give them a gift that they weren't capable of giving me years before, acceptance.

After the conference it felt like I had passed a test I didn't know I was taking. For every time I ran away or sunk into myself when I was rejected, that was the one time I'd stand my ground. Having the support of my brother helped and I enjoyed the moment. As much as I basked in that moment, a floating thought came into my head that startled me. I was able to break through a huge barrier in my life through my relationship with God and with the support of my brother, but I was also shown that the day would come where I'd have to break through another barrier without his support, without anyone's support. There would come a time where I couldn't just be the little brother anymore. I'd have to be something else, something more. That startled me because being the little brother was all I'd ever known and I didn't know what it was to be anything else, nor did I desire it.

I shook my head to regulate my thoughts and stay in the moment as we were celebrating a successful weekend. I had a tendency to fly away with my thoughts when I'm supposed to be present in a moment. I could hear and feel everything that was going on around me, but I wouldn't interact with it because my thoughts were elsewhere. That's always been fascinating to me. I could repeat everything you said to me while I'm calculating how many steps it takes to get from Atlanta to Austin on foot.

A few days later, my brother asked me to go on a tour with him right before telling me that he was starting his own church. "That's what it was!" I shouted in my head. That's what I was seeing in him that I couldn't articulate to him. That new characteristic was him detaching from where he was so he could get to where he was going. I immediately asked what he needed help with. He told me he was having a meeting in the first week of July to talk about it. "I'm already there." My relationship with church was a bit fractured, but my brother never had to ask twice for my support.

SATURDAY JULY 8, 1995

Fresh off of being kicked out of summer camp for fighting, I was playing in our neighborhood. 15 hummingbird court was one of our childhood homes I remember the most. We did quite a bit of moving. Our parents were determined to get me and Mark out of the city of Baltimore, so they did everything in their power to make that a reality. The unfortunate part about that is it caused me to have to attend six different elementary schools and three high schools. Anytime I would get attached to a place, it'd be ripped away from me because we were moving so much. That made it difficult to make friends and began to smother my desire to even try. 15 hummingbird court was the longest we lived anywhere in Baltimore. Three and a half years.

I was being bullied in summer camp and I was doing my best to ignore the bully. I didn't even remember his name or what he looked like. All I remember is blood. In the camp, we were separated by grade, so I wasn't able to be in the same camp class as my brother. I don't know why the kid wanted to bully me, but he was bothering me all morning. When it was time for lunch, we all went to the gym to play, and he still wouldn't stop. All I could think in my head was, "don't hit them first. I don't care what they say to you, do not hit them first." Our parents drilled that into our heads. I kept my composure even though I could feel the white-hot surge forming in my body, and then boom! He hit me. I remember being happy that he hit me. I smiled and then I charged at him. Everything went bright white and then black. "I must have closed my eyes for a long time," I thought to myself. When I looked down, the kid was lying on the ground bloodied, crying, seething in pain. The camp leaders rushed to grab me as I un-balled my fists, releasing strands of hair and blood from my fingertips. Everyone in the camp saw it but me. I overheard my brother explaining what happened to my parents. From his and everyone else's perspective, once the kid hit me, I punched him in the face so hard it backed him into the corner of the bleachers. He then tried to run away but I grabbed him and threw him against the bleachers headfirst, continuously smashing his forehead against it until he fell to the ground. I didn't remember any of it and I didn't know enough to be concerned. I only saw it as defending myself, but I clearly took it too far. I was banned from the camp indefinitely.

I was on punishment and the only time I could go out and play was on the weekends. I planned to take full advantage of my time. I went outside at about 7am and played until the sun reached its highest and hottest. I collected caterpillars, raced some kids in the neighborhood and went over to my friend, Young Sam's house to play video games. Around noon, I came back outside to go to the candy lady who lived up the street from us at 41

Hummingbird court. I loved her frozen cups. I was in such a hurry, I accidently knocked over someone's bike. "Oh, my bad," I picked the bike back up and put it on the stand. The kid loudly addressed me. "I should beat yo ass for that, yo." He was a bit older than me and bigger than me, but nothing about him said that I couldn't take him easily. The fact that he wanted to bring so much attention to us by screaming so loud let me know that he didn't really want a fight. He just wanted to punk me in front of everyone. That wasn't uncommon in our neighborhood, especially for newcomers and I could tell that he was new. I ignored him, but he kept screaming. He got closer to me. "Please don't touch me," I thought to myself. I was already in trouble, and I don't like to see disappointment in my parents' faces. I kept my cool and smiled. He pushed me as hard as he could, but it didn't move me. I walked to the front porch of the candy lady house and sat down. I felt myself getting hot and needed to sit down before I did anything that I couldn't remember. "Oh, you scared, huh?" He clearly couldn't read a room. I was trying to save him, but he was too focused on gaining a reputation that he wouldn't be able to enjoy. I put my head down, "I said, 'my bad'. Leave me alone." He didn't listen. He walked up to me, took his pointer and middle finger and slapped it against the left side of my face. That white hot surge covered my body again and fighting against it frustrated me. I wanted to fight, I enjoyed it, but I knew I couldn't get in any more trouble. Plus, I couldn't trust myself to not go too far anymore. Instead of anger, I felt frustration and it brought tears to my eyes.

To have the ability to crush someone and choose to not do it… I think I just figured out how to love as an eight-year-old. It didn't feel good, so I cried. The kid must have felt 10 feet tall as he stepped back smiling in pride. That feeling didn't last long at all because as he made his final step back, a fist glided through the right side of his jaw. My brother didn't share the same resolve as I did. He wailed on the new kid from one side of the street to the other. It was so bad that with every punch, he launched the kid backwards until he fell on his back leaving himself open for attack. My brother had no remorse; he kept attacking. Coincidentally, they found themselves in front of my uncle and his girlfriend's house. Uncle Corey ran out and tried to pull Mark off of the kid. At 6 foot 6 inches 220lbs, Uncle Corey had trouble getting Mark off the kid. Once he finally picked Mark up, he carried him all the way home as Mark kept kicking and screaming for Uncle Corey to let him go so he could finish the job. Uncle Corey couldn't help but laugh. The kid stumbled to get up and walked into the house Uncle Corey just came out of. The kid was Uncle Corey's girlfriend's nephew. Small world. Uncle Corey explained to our parents what happened and now both of us were on punishment. We didn't care. Me and my brothers' relationship was forged in love, protection, support and violence. We were raised to be there for each other, even if it got us in trouble with the people who raised us.

JUNE 2009

I'd been on a tour before, but instead of my destination being the local strip club it was now the local church. My brother had created a campaign called "Dreaming Out Loud" to which the tagline expressed to everyone that hope was the audacity to dream out loud. I loved that, especially since that pretty much summed up me and God's car conversations. My life would be dedicated to opening and revealing the dreams inside of people and inside of myself by using my artistic expression. I wish I could find the flier of Mark, Korey Bowie and Darlene McCoy's faces plastered on a cloud-like background with their names embossed on it. I produced, wrote and recorded a song for the tour called "Hope". I was always gifted at embodying a theme into a song. I've been in front of so many different crowds. I've been in front of strip club crowds, nightclub crowds, church crowds, corporate crowds, even school crowds. They're all so similar. They're just people who desire a transfer of energy from the person in front of them. I don't care if you're giving a speech, preaching, singing, rapping, dancing, acting, doing spoken word or anything on a stage, the questions are always the same. Can you make these people feel? Can you make them think? Can you flip a switch inside of them that provokes them to move? Can you turn a light on in the iris of their dulling eyes? No matter what crowd it is, we're all the same.

We got back in town just in time to go to the meeting. There were about twenty of us inside of a Hyatt hotel conference room. I sat next to my brother's best friend, Charles. We were about 15 minutes into the meeting when I realized I had nothing to offer for his new church. I knew nothing about the inner workings of church. I was totally oblivious. You walk in, the people are singing. After the singing comes the preaching, then they ask for the offering and then everyone goes home. That was the extent of my church service knowledge. I was clearly in the wrong room, but I listened anyway. The meeting felt like a baseball game, it was so exciting. Again, Marquis Derrell Lamar Donte Boone was gravity.

People spoke about how excited they were and how they couldn't wait for the first service. Even though I didn't share everyone else's excitement, I was proud to be a part of something my brother was doing. We got to the part of the meeting where everyone explained what area they would volunteer in. I heard 'praise team', I heard 'greeting', I heard 'prayer', I heard 'finance'. None of it piqued my interest. Then they got around to Charles. He fixed his glasses to his face and leaned forward in his chair, "I'll do IT support." "Me too," I blurted out before he explained. I had no idea what IT support was, but it sounded like I could learn without being around people. The meeting was over and everyone was having side conversations inside of the conference room. A woman approached me, small in stature, about 4ft 10 inches, but her voice was 10ft tall. When she spoke, she did so with a confidence that couldn't be faked. She walked right up to me and tilted her head upward to lock eyes with me. Grabbing my hands, she squeezed them as if she had answers to questions I hadn't asked yet. "Everyone here is praying for your brother. I'm praying for you, and I'll keep praying for you no matter where I am." She spoke as if she knew something she couldn't tell me. "Thank you, Ms Koran." It was all I could think to say. She pulled me down to her and gave me a hug, kissed me on the cheek, pulled back gently, smiled and walked away. I haven't seen her since that day. With everyone now in the parking lot, someone screamed from the inside of their car, "Boone! What's going to be the name of the church?" My brother used his childlike smile, raised his palms to the side of his face and bellowed out, "Fresh Start! Fresh Start Church!"

8. CRAWLING BACK

MONDAY DECEMBER 21, 2009

I had been contemplating for a few months. Driving up i-285 North, I was terrified, excited and anxious to the point of tears. It was the day I put in my two weeks' notice at Macy's. The agreement God and I made was once I made enough money to build my studio, I would quit Macy's so I could record my mixtape and start my studio company. I built my studio back in June, but I was too comfortable to move on. I got used to waking up in time to make it to work by 9am and getting off at 5pm. I got used to fitting my life around my work schedule. I got used to being normal and respected amongst my peers for having a 'real' job. I got used to fitting in again, being invisible, and I didn't want to give that up. I was proud of the life that I was able to create over the past year, but I mistook it for something permanent rather than the temporary and necessary step I needed to take for where I was going. That was a pattern that would torment me until I turned 28. Tell me if you relate:

There would be parts of my journey where I'd be given a task to complete. The task would take as long as it took, and I would complete it. Once the task was complete, I'd do it again and again and again instead of moving on. I'd stay in that place as long as I could because it brought me comfort and stability. For someone who had anything but stability growing up from moving so much, I yearned for it. I knew how to complete the task and I could do it with my eyes closed. Long story short, I'd stay in places longer than I needed to because I enjoyed the consistency of it, sometimes to my detriment. I did that with my career, relationships and my purpose. I yearned for consistency and stability, but the ambition inside of me yearned for growth. That meant change, that meant movement. That also meant stability and comfort was an opposing force to my growth, change and movement. My struggle with those two ideals ruined a lot of relationships in my life. Consistency, stability and comfort are huge parts of any and every type of relationship. Although I desired to be and experience those things, almost everything inside of me pulled toward the opposite direction and I always felt bad about that. I wanted a normal life, but everything in and about me was far from it.

The comfort side of me wanted to continue working at Macy's. I convinced myself I could make everything else work around it. The ambitious side of me knew I'd never be happy staying there. Experiencing that made me appreciate my parents. It gave me empathy for them. Every time we moved to a new home, I'd go kicking and screaming because I didn't want to go. My parents made that decision because their objective was to have a better life for their children. They cared about my feelings, but my growth was far more important to them. Driving to Macy's that day, I understood that, because now I'd have to make that decision for myself. They couldn't make it for me anymore.

As I was getting off exit 29 Ashford Dunwoody, I was going over in my mind what I was going to say to my manager, Terrence, when tears started dropping out of my eyes. I wouldn't have noticed it had the tears not dropped onto my right arm as I turned into the Perimeter Mall parking lot. I walked onto the dock to clock in when I was greeted by Mike. He had already started limiting his hours on the job, but I intended on making a clean break. I was looking for Terrence, but I didn't see him. "Hey, James! I need you on the truck gettin' those boxes!" Derrick shouted from across the dock room. Terrence was our manager, but Derrick was our supervisor. He ran the entire dock.

Terrence ran the department. I skipped toward the truck greeting all of my coworkers on the way. "Anybody seen Terrence?" Mike was in the truck with me. "He on the floor. He should be back down in a sec once the store opens." Mike started out as a dock hand, but as time went along Terrence and Derrick began trusting him with shipping. He began working more closely with them so if anyone knew where Terrence was, it was Mike. Maybe 30 minutes later, Terrence came strutting into the dock area giving instructions to anyone who would listen. Terrence spoke at such a fast pace that sounded as if he was stuttering. It didn't help that he walked just as fast while he spoke, so he made one lap around the dock and was on his way back out. I heard his voice from the inside of the truck; I came running out tripping over the boxes I just laid out. "Terrence, wait up!" He was already at the elevator. "Hey, what up James!" Terrence always liked to stand straight up and stick his chest out whenever around anyone taller than his 5 ft 5-inch frame. I never minded, I understood.

I don't remember the words I used, but I let Terrence know I was putting in my two weeks' notice to start my own business. He showed disappointment but he congratulated me. He asked if I could stay until the 20th of January to get through the holiday season; I was ok with that. Terrence had always been good to me, so it was no problem. Before he got onto the elevator, he told me that I'd always have a job with him; I'd only need to ask. I appreciated that, but I had no intention of coming back. The elevator lifted and I went back to work.

SUNDAY OCTOBER 17, 2010

The church had been doing well from what I saw. I wasn't very well versed in church culture, but I could tell that this was different. It wasn't a normal church. You could dress how you wanted. Service was different each time. Everything had a theme. It felt fresh. We had been on the move for the past year. We started out having services at the Gwinnett performing arts arena. A few months after, we moved to a 7th Day Adventists church. It was less expensive and more sustainable for the growth of the church. It was a genius idea to rent it out, especially since the 7th Day Adventists used their church for Saturday services. We ended up getting our own building just in time for our 1-year anniversary and we started to pick up steam. We were a church full of rejects who all connected on the premise that we didn't belong in the conventional church culture. That's how we grew, not only with each other, but with God.

I'd never really been a fan of gospel music. If it wasn't Fred Hammond or Israel Houghton, I wouldn't pay too much attention to it. Anytime I heard gospel music I only heard begging and desperation, for the most part. Not all of it, but enough of it that I began to recognize a pattern. I heard the same when I listened to people pray. For me it was reminiscent of slavery, as if we'd forgotten that we weren't slaves anymore. As a performer, I was all for provoking emotion. Somehow, when I listened to gospel music, it felt like an abuse of that emotion. It also felt like a dependence on that emotion. From what I've learned about God, I don't think He breathed breath into the bodies of beggars, especially if said bodies were made in His image. Before I got too judgmental about my opinion, I had to stop myself. Image. I recognized a huge discrepancy in the way different cultures worshiped God through music in comparison to us.

5:57am MONDAY JUNE 6, 2022

I was climbing Stone Mountain with my godbrother, Aj. He's a musical savant. When he first started singing, he was rather terrible though. That lasted for years, but he never stopped trying. Usually, when someone tried to sing, there was some sort of potential for their voice to keep going. For Aj, there was none. No one would have been surprised if he just stopped. In fact, everyone's surprise was that he kept trying. Aj willed himself to sing and sing well. He sang so well that he was sought after by just about every church in the region. He learned, he studied and obsessed over everything having to do with worshiping God through music. He also studied under the musical genius of Korey Bowie.

We made it to the top of the mountain 40 minutes before the sun rose. On that morning, we walked by two Caucasian women who were already at the top of the mountain. They were listening to a song called "So Will I" by Hillsong Worship. The song was beautiful, but I was bothered. Covered by the darkness of the sky only lit by the stars, I turned to Aj and asked, "why is it that white people's worship music sounds like they're in the sky flying and ours sound like we're on the ground begging?"

We spoke about it and even began to research it until after the sun came up. Aj explained how singing with different cultures opened his eyes to what our motives were when we worshiped. Culturally, white people have had the privilege of worshiping God in a freedom that black Americans struggled to attain psychologically. They were inspired to worship God. We were desperate to. That desperation contributed to how we worshiped God through music. The lyrics, the tones, the instruments, the frequencies were all altered by our lowly perspectives of ourselves. Image. Since any of us could remember, Jesus was portrayed as a European-looking white man. Even though Jesus was described as middle eastern, bronzed skin and coarse haired, we believed that He was a white man who looked nothing like us. Image. Psychologically, if Jesus looked like the people who enslaved us, then we'd naturally see ourselves the way the people who enslaved us did. That revealed itself through generations of music. We sang to endure the burdens of slavery. We sang desperate for freedom. We sang for scraps. We sang for the approval of those who enslaved us. We sang for God to bless us with money because we had none. We sang like slaves because that's what we saw ourselves to be. Image. Because we were lied to about what our savior looked like, we believed that we were meant to be beggars. Even when we rejected that notion outwardly, we still internally struggled with it. It would be revealed to us that it was engineered that way by the enemy, because if he could get us to believe that we were a lower version of ourselves, we'd never fulfill the potential of who we truly were.

As black people, especially black Americans with seemingly no connection to our true heritage, we'd spiritually and psychologically battle against self-image for generations. I understood that until we could confront that portion of our faith, we'd transactionally treat our relationship with God similar to our relationship with our former slave masters. From where Aj and I sat, we could no longer afford to accept business as usual when it came to how we worshiped God.

SUNDAY OCTOBER 17, 2010

I always kept that opinion to myself until Korey Bowie, musical genius and now our worship pastor, presented an idea to us in rehearsal. A worship pastor is pretty much the leader of all things music in the church. He introduced us to the difference between 'God centered worship' and 'me centered worship'. The 'me centered worship' were the songs that focused most on the person, how we feel, what we're going through and how that connects with God. The 'God centered worship' were songs that focused most on God, who He is, what He does and how He connects with us. Korey said that we wanted to focus more on God centered worship because the opposite runs the risk of us making the music, the worship about us rather than about God.

His position was that 'me centered worship' wasn't a bad thing, but if we were going to make an impact on people, we had to be able to let them know that God was bigger than anything and everything. Our focus was to be on Him and trusting that His focus would be on us. I loved that concept because it not only made sense to me, it also made me feel like what I was thinking wasn't exactly crazy. Korey and my brother had a vision of blending Christian Contemporary Music with gospel voices creating a fusion sound that wouldn't be subject to culture, race or ethnicity. As a kid who grew up with a father who loved Baby Face, Bruce Springsteen, Bob Marley, Tracy Chapman, Biggie Smalls, Shania Twain, New Edition, Prince and Hootie and The Blowfish, it was music heaven for me.

Up until that point, I hadn't been moved by church music. It hadn't provoked an interaction with God for me the way I've seen it for everyone else every Sunday. On that Sunday, the praise team, these are the people who sing the songs, themed their songs around the word 'Holy'. Holy means to be separated as sacred and pure. We'd spend that Sunday expressing how sacred and pure we found God to be. I was used to experiencing and facilitating other people's interaction with God from the outside looking in. This, however, would be a moment for me. They sang 3 songs. From my perspective, the first two were business as usual. I engineered the sound; Stephanie ran the presentation of the words on the screen and Christina operated the lights from the left wall. As a media team we were in sync. Korey would have it no other way. He was adamant about us being just as important to the experience as the people on stage. The lights were a deep blue, giving a resemblance of an open sky during the blue hour. The words on the screen followed each melody sung by the praise team and it sounded like we were in a private concert for angels.

The third song started. I heard the guitar strumming a rhythm similar to a bird calling in the forest. Even though I heard the song in rehearsal, it made me feel different that Sunday. I raised my head away from the sound board to the stage in an awe I'd never felt before. Korey began singing the lyrics, "you are king. You are lord. You are mighty, God. You are holy." Those are all the words to the song and those were the only words I needed to have my own personal experience with God through song. It's commonly known as worship, but as the praise team was singing, I sang along, and I imagined what it would feel like to be so pure and so sacred that it separates you from the rest of reality. It brought me to tears as I kneeled to the ground and sprawled onto the floor. I wasn't thinking, I wasn't wandering. I wasn't even there. One by one everything and everyone disappeared until it was only me in this deep blue room alone with God. I could still hear the music, yet all I saw were the words of the song glowing and floating around me while creating this promised land of space between me and God. It felt like I was there all day, but when I came to the song was still playing. I believe everyone has a song that does that for them. For me, it was a song called "Holy" by C3 Oxford Falls.

SATURDAY JULY 2, 2011

Entrepreneurship had broken me. It broke me mentally, financially, spiritually, 'everythingly'. I was helping a friend of mine move into their new house. My heart ached. My nerves were shot. I couldn't think straight. I was bringing in a large box and placed it on the office floor when my legs gave out. I fell to the ground. I wasn't physically fatigued, but my emotions felt like weighted vests all over my body. I lied there wondering what happened to me. 2010 was a great year for me. I had steady clients. I was hosting a weekly studio party called "Mixtape Saturdays", also called "Patron Saturdays" as an inside joke. I was releasing more music projects that I was proud of. Everything seemed to be going in the right direction. I thought I had safeguarded myself from my past mistakes I'd made in business. I had contracts for clients, and an additional hard drive in case my computer malfunctions. I even had a schedule setup for my workflow. But nothing could safe guard me from clients no longer showing up.

In late January, after the snowstorm coined "Snowmageddon", I was behind on client work because all of the roads were shut down. I had a client that requested I master his group's new record for a club performance. Rushing through it, I mastered the song and sent it straight to the client so I could get back to a bigger, more time-consuming project. I neglected to listen to the song after I exported it. An export is when you take the work you've done and turn it into an mp3 so you could listen on any device. I normally ear tested the song in the studio, in the car and on a sound system before sending it to a client. I failed to do that. If I had, I would have recognized that I accidently raised the bass of the song 5db too high. The client was already one of the more erratic clients, so he called me and let me have it. He let me know the bass was so high that no one could hear the vocals in the club for their performance. "Why do you have vocals on a performance track, anyway?" I thought to myself. That wasn't the point, though. I was rushing through my client's work, work that I prided myself on taking extra care of. The client told everyone he knew. It black balled me out of that client circle, a circle I depended on for income. I had major plans for the year 2011, plans that included an actual album, business expansion and a marriage proposal to my girlfriend. I even had a few record deals on the table. I needed the income.

Weeks and then months went by as I scraped by getting as many clients as I could to supplement the income lost, while working double to then try to expand my reach. I exhausted myself and it seemed as if I was getting nowhere. "But I got promises to keep," I kept telling myself each time I felt myself getting sleepy. When I did succumb to sleep, I did so with the thought, "maybe you need to just get a job to make these things happen." It was happening again. The comfort side of me knew that breaking down and getting a job somewhere would provide me the necessary resources to do what I desired. After all, no woman is going to be with a man who cannot provide consistency, stability, security and comfort, nor should they. The ambitious side of me screamed, "we're almost there! Something big is close to happening. Keep going!" I wanted the comfort and stability, but I also wanted the things I knew my ambition could provide. I fought with it for so long because I had no idea how to merge the two, and I couldn't reconcile that maybe they're not meant to merge. These were powerful and conflicting thoughts that I never shared. When I woke up in the mornings after having those conflicting thoughts as I slept every night, I got back to work. I hadn't chosen definitively which part of me was most important, but I learned that if you wait long enough, decisions have a way of making themselves. The deals didn't happen. The album didn't happen. The proposal didn't go well.

Entrepreneurship had broken me. Lying on the floor I began thinking, "this wouldn't have happened if I stayed safe, in my comfort, in my stability. I wouldn't be here if I would have just stayed at Macy's." I pulled out my phone. I could usually talk this kind of stuff out with Mark or mommy. I went to my favorite contacts and pressed 9. The phone was dialing, and I was trying to think of how I'd start the conversation. They answered the phone, "Hey, James." The voice spoke to me. "Hey, uh, can I speak to, is Terrence available?" I hated every word that came out of my mouth. "Sure, one sec," when they put me on hold I thought of 100 reasons for me to just hang up. "Hello," Terrence came to the phone making the word 'hello' sound like one syllable with his fast and excited speech. "Hey, Terrence. It's James. How you doin'?" I tried to match his enthusiasm. "What's up, man! How's everything going? How's business?" His questions felt like daggers to my throat. "Um, not so good. That's why I'm calling. I was wondering if you still had a spot open for me on the dock." I was embarrassed and I sounded like it. I tried to mask it but I didn't have the energy to. "You called me just in time. I'm about to transfer to another store, but I can try to get you back in up here at the Perimeter location if you want. Just go online and fill the application out again so we can find you in the system." Terrence spoke the type of assurance that said he'd been awaiting my call. It wasn't in an arrogant 'I knew you'd be back' way. It was like he'd seen this before, like I'm not the first person to try and go out on my own only to come crawling back. He'd given this speech before, and he wasn't judgmental about it. It didn't make me feel any better, I wish it did. I thanked him and hung up the phone. Opening the internet browser on my blackberry I typed in www.macys.com and searched for the careers tab as I had done two and a half years prior. I opened the application page and it asked for my name. I bursted into tears.

"Is this what trusting God looks like?" I began thinking about what filling this job application meant for me. I failed to get a record deal. I failed my relationship. I failed to expand my business. But does that mean everything is over? Me filling out the job application would indicate that it's over. I'd be going back to what made me comfortable. I'd be going back to what was easy. I'd be going back to what was safe. If I fill out the job application, then everything I rapped about was a lie. Every sentence I wrote about following your dreams would be folly. Everything that I went through to get where I was meant nothing. If I fill out the job application, I don't believe God. But it hurts, failure hurts. It's embarrassing. Living below the life I dreamed is embarrassing too. Knowing I could have done better and didn't hurt more than almost anything. I bursted into tears because as badly as I wanted to go back to Macy's, I wanted the life God told me about in the car more. As much as I wanted to be safe, I've only ever grown being dangerous. As much as I'd go kicking and screaming, it's the path I always chose. I couldn't fill the application out. I closed my phone, put it in my pocket and continued helping my friend move. Once I made it outside, my phone rang. I was asked to run sound for my brother and mega artist Tasha Cobbs' mini tour the next week.

9. PRAYER & PROPHECY

PRESENT

Sound is something I'm naturally great at. I would obsess over every sound I could hear in order to be a better sound guy. I was also pushed to become a better sound guy by Korey. He helped tune my ears, not to notes, but to sound itself. Sound had always fascinated me, it moved me. I had been running sound since the beginning of Fresh Start. Before then, I had never run live sound in my life. I loved music and I didn't want to volunteer anywhere else at the church so sound chose me as much as I chose it. With any equipment, I could fill a room with sound pleasing to everyone's ears because of my obsession with it. I could see sound in full color, watch it move and guide it to where it needed to go.

I was rather self-deprecating when it came to the gifts I possess. I tended to assume that my gifts were easily possessed by others, therefore depreciating the value of them. I assumed that the things that I could do, others could too. It's because I do those things without thinking. I saw sound without thinking. I operated sound without thinking. I wrote without thinking. I rapped without thinking. I created without thinking. I thought without thinking. It just happened and since it came so easy for me, my assumption was that it must be the same for everyone else. I was wrong about that and each time I subjected myself to that type of thinking, I operated below where God placed me. I thought it was a lack of confidence but the more I discovered about myself I realized it was my ignorance and lack of introspection. I spent so much of my life watching other people, I rarely took time to examine myself. Thankfully, God would send people I could trust to make some of those examinations for me until I could do them myself.

TUESDAY MAY 24, 2011

Exhausted from trying to service as many clients as possible while revitalizing my reputation as an audio engineer, I laid across the chairs lined up in the sound booth at the church. We'd been doing this new thing for us called Fresh Groups where we'd separate into different classes based upon different subjects. There were about 6 classes in total. I was tasked with operating sound for the Prayer & Prophetic class. I had never heard of it before, so I was intrigued to see what it was about. Around 6pm, an hour before everything started, I was still stretched out across the chairs by the sound board when a lady came walking into the sanctuary. Slim, short haircut with a childlike face, she cleaned her glasses as she walked up to me. "Hi, let me ask you something. Do you feel a lot of frustration about your music not being accepted by churches?" I don't remember seeing this lady before, but she spoke to me as if we'd crossed paths before. She spoke to emotions I felt for years that hadn't been reconciled. She began telling me about things I'd do because of my rejection that would reveal why the rejection was necessary.

After she spoke, she just walked away. I was frozen, taken aback and a little excited at the same time. That was something else I never experienced before. I'd seen it happen to other people, but I never thought about it happening to me. It's called 'Prophecy'. It's the ability to reveal a partial future of someone's life directly from God. The class was created to teach the students how to use it, what it's used for, how prayer is connected to it and how not to abuse it. The class was taught by Sonya Cruel and Carol Sherard. The idea of the class scared me a bit, just enough to get me interested to pay attention. Even though I wasn't in the class, I got to see everything. That's a perk of being the sound guy.

That day was special. Coming into the end of the semester, the class was used to test what the students had been learning all year. Each student would line up on the right side of the wall while the teachers picked someone from a different class at random. Whoever was picked would stand in the front of the class and each student, one by one, would have to present a prophecy to the person. I remember thinking to myself that I'd be a wreck if I was a student in that class. My nerves would be shot. They went up there one by one as each random person was chosen and they used their gift to the best of their ability. The teachers even brought outside guests to help assist the students along while in the process. It was amazing to watch. Sonya was walking up the center aisle toward the soundboard. She had this way of walking and bobbing her head back and forth in rhythm while her hands were clasped together half covering her face when things got intense for her. She continued walking and stopped in front of the sound booth. She lifted her head a bit and her eyes met mine as I was sitting and pretending to adjust the sound, "please don't call on me," I said to myself. "Would you mind us using you next?" She spoke with a medium whisper ensuring that I heard her. "Damnit!" My thought was so loud I thought she heard it when her eyebrows rose. My exclamation wasn't of resistance or rebellion. It was out of fear of being the center of attention, "Yes." I stood anyway and prepared myself to walk to the front. What I heard sent shockwaves through my soul.

A prophecy isn't a guarantee, after all it's our actions that determine the outcome. It also doesn't mean that what's being said will happen the very next day. God isn't subject to time no matter how much we try to encapsulate Him in it. Throughout the Bible, anytime prophecy was used, its purpose was to change the faith and behavior of the people who received it. It was to give encouragement. It was to give instruction. It was also to give correction. I had no idea, then.

I went to bed that night thinking I was going to be rich by the time I woke up. When I woke up, I was trying to figure out what it all meant. I wanted a studio company, not multiple businesses. It was exciting but also overwhelming. Three things stuck out to me: everyone said great things, but the woman 2nd to last told me that it was important that I read my word, that's the Bible. If I was going to experience all the things these people were speaking over me, I'd have to read my word more often so I could hear God's voice clearer. It was ironic because, at the time, I'd been so consumed with my work that I neglected my time spent with God. My car rides were getting fewer and further from one another. Even after hearing her say that I continued consuming myself in my work without God's help. The second thing that stuck out was Carol, I call her mama Carol. She was last. As soon as she said, 'come out of hiding' I wanted to sink in my seat. I loved to hide. I had never enjoyed people looking at me. The center of attention made me uncomfortable because I feared scrutiny, criticism and attention itself. I had gotten so used to being invisible that being seen felt foreign. The last thing that stuck out to me was when Shelly spoke to me about tuning my ear to spiritual things the same way I naturally tune my ear to the soundboard. Sound was always something I used to make sense of everything around me. To be told that the things I do with natural sound, I can also do with spiritual things overwhelmed me. It felt like I was given a new complicated toy with no instruction manual on how to use it. And with me being unwilling to risk breaking it, I didn't play with it at all. I just let it stay where it was inside of me and continued doing whatever I was doing.

10. "CAN I SEE YOU
IN MY OFFICE PLEASE?"

MONDAY JANUARY 2, 2012

Nothing could have prepared me for that day. My hands were shaking. My mind was racing. Everything felt like it was going 100 miles an hour, yet I was standing still. Music blaring out of the next room, I sat in a director's chair with Joe at my back taking pictures. Joe and I are godbrothers. It was 7:03 pm and we're getting ready for my first album release party. After losing everything over the summer, I locked myself in the studio to complete my album and called it "The Terminator". The album was dedicated to terminating the fear, doubt, worry and disbelief in our lives so we could chase after our dreams unencumbered. I asked for the help of the people I admired most with the album. Mike did my graphics. Kenneth Paryo, my producer since I started, produced most of the album. Anything that wasn't produced by him was produced by Korey Bowie and one song was produced by me and another god brother of mine, Antonio Cunningham. After a few features and interludes, the album was ready.

Kenneth was hosting the party all night and kept people energized. After about an hour of mingling, Kenneth called me to the stage. It was a milestone and I soaked in every moment of it. I performed songs from the album under a strobe light, proclaiming motivation and inspiration as the base message of my work. It was so dark that I couldn't see anyone. I only heard cheers and singing along which made me feel like I was doing a good job. 45 minutes had passed, just like I rehearsed it, and I concluded the concert. The lights came on and I got to see all the faces of the people who showed up for me. I was floored. Friends, family, musician acquaintances all came to celebrate this accomplishment with me.

PRESENT

I didn't know it then, but that would be the start of a long and windy road for me. A road in which a lot of it had nothing to do with my music but with the words embedded inside of it. My first love was not business. My first love was not film. My first love was not sound. My first love was not even music. My first love was language. Words mean everything to me and I'm a believer that words create and destroy everything according to our use of them. That's why I use so little of them whether I'm speaking or writing. I believe each word is so powerful that we don't need fillers. Words and the expression of them have always been my North Star. I loved the way words paint pictures. I loved how they create songs, scripts and stories. I loved how they make people feel when used in love. And I loved that I'll never be able to discover all of them in my lifetime. What I don't particularly love and what I didn't count on was me being called on to use them so much.

SUNDAY SEPTEMBER 30, 2012

Ever since releasing my album, I'd been really busy with performances and interviews. As an independent artist, staying in front of people was necessary for growth. I used every opportunity I could to perform and speak about my album and I could feel the expansion of my efforts. In the middle of the year, I was approached by a company called Tate Music Group about a distribution and marketing deal. Distribution is the act of getting your music to the people and marketing is the promotion strategies of that music. I consulted my brother about the deal, and he thought it was fair. It was a huge benefit to me because distributing your own music was time consuming and marketing is a full-time job in which I didn't have the time or skill to acquire. Anything that could help me to remain focused on the music, I was drawn to it. A stipulation of the deal was that I would have to remix and master the album again to make it industry standard. That would take even more time because I did all of my mixing and mastering. The work was overwhelming, but it was the work I loved. I'd wake up early in the morning to knock out my client work. Next, I'd look up and book places to perform. Then I'd promote songs from my album on my Twitter and Facebook. After that I'd do some recording for any new ideas I had. Last, I'd end the night by remixing and mastering the songs from my Terminator album. The label wanted to re-release it in November, so I was really working against the clock. Every day was the same schedule. I was focused. I was persistent. I was obsessed. I was also missing something.

I was spending so much time on my music that I forgot about my responsibilities elsewhere. I had become the media director at the church. That just meant I was over everything audio and visual at the church. That was inclusive of sound, lighting, video, presentation and maintenance of those things. We were in our third year of operating so it was natural that things would begin to need maintenance in the electronics area. It was a new experience for me altogether. Although I knew how to operate the equipment, I had no idea how to fix it if anything went wrong. Our left loudspeaker went out on us during a service and I was in charge of getting it repaired or replaced. After a consultation from the guys who installed the speakers, we found out that a tweeter was blown in the speaker. A tweeter is the part of the speaker that pushes out the high frequencies in the sound. Certain sounds in the piano, guitar, cymbals and other instruments were tough to hear with the tweeter being out and it created an imbalance that made it unpleasant to listen to. I ordered the new tweeter and learned how to replace it. Over the weekend, before Sunday, I was supposed to replace the tweeter so we could be set to go for service. Well, I forgot. I had been forgetting a lot of things lately, especially with my obsession to the details in my music career. That was my brain again; I obsessed and then nothing else existed anymore.

As media director, I was usually the first person in the building on Sunday mornings. I walked in and looked to see the face of the speaker missing. That reminded me that I had forgotten to replace the tweeter. I ran to the back to grab the tweeter and a ladder so I could hurry and replace it before Korey came in. When I ran to the back, I saw that Korey's office door was open. "Shit!" I thought to myself. A bit of shame hovered over me as I grabbed the tweeter and the ladder. It took almost 30 minutes for me to replace the tweeter since it was my first time doing it alone. The band and the praise team had to wait on me to finish before they could rehearse. Korey was furious. At the time we had three services, 7:30am, 9am and 11am.

We were in the middle of the third service when my phone vibrated. I looked at my phone and sighed louder than I intended. Christina, our lighting and presentation specialist chuckled, "he texted you to come to his office after service, didn't he?" Everyone knew what a text message from Korey in mid service meant. "Meet me in my office after service, please." We've all gotten that text message before. It meant we were about to be in trouble. Korey's brand of excellence was much different from Darrick or Meca. They demanded excellence in effort. Korey demanded excellence in execution. If it wasn't operated properly and at the highest level possible, Korey would have something to say about it. As scary or unattainable as that may seem, I respected that, and I counted on it to keep me in line and focused.

As service ended, I made my way to Korey's office. I walked in and he ripped the Band-Aid off, "James, I'm sitting you down." The phrase 'sitting you down' is church talk for being suspended from duty. It shocked me, but I couldn't say I was surprised. Throughout the three services, I was thinking about all the things I had let slip through the cracks for the most part of the year in my area. I couldn't believe I'd been so oblivious to it before then. He spoke to me as if it hurt him to say those things to me. I thought he was suspending me because I waited so long to fix the speaker. The reality was that the speaker was just the last straw. If I remember his words correctly, he was suspending me because as media director I hadn't led the media team to grow. From Korey's perspective, the issue wasn't that the speaker was fixed so late. The issue was I had a team of 5 people and I was still doing everything myself.

My team leaned on me to do everything, not because they were incapable, but because I never taught them. He kept speaking and I sat down in front of him. He was right. I hadn't worked on or led a team since the step team 6 years ago. Even though I was given a leadership role, I had no idea how to lead. I knew how to work and produce a great service and product. I didn't know how to recreate that same work inside of someone else. "Your team is going to have to figure out how to make this work without you for a while. In the meantime, I want you to start learning how to become a better leader. I know you can, but not like this." With every word, Korey was kicking me out, but it didn't feel like rejection. It felt like a correction. He recommended some books for me to read and told me from then until the end of the year, I wasn't allowed to go to the media booth. That was the only thing in church that I loved, and it was being taken away from me. The odd part about it is that I felt relieved. Korey didn't know it, but he opened a passion inside of me that made no sense to me. I wanted to become a leader, a good leader, a great leader. I had always been given leadership roles according to the work I could do, but I was never given a role based on my ability to lead. I didn't know how to lead, but I was going to find out.

MONDAY DECEMBER 24, 2012

While I was suspended, my eyes were open to so many things that I wouldn't be able to see otherwise. It had been three years since I had been able to just go to church without working, years longer since I actually sat in a service. My first time walking into service without anything to do was beyond awkward. I sat down trying to turn my brain off of work mode, but I kept hearing things I could fix. I kept seeing things I could fix, and I wanted to fix them. That showed me why I was in the position I was in. I wanted to fix everything and each time I did, I robbed the people I led from learning to see what I saw. I fixed; I didn't teach.

As the weeks went along, I got more comfortable with seeing a mess without feeling obligated to be the one to fix it. And the longer I wasn't there to fix it, the more someone else would fill in the gap. It didn't have to be all on me and I had to learn which assignments belonged to me while not touching the ones that didn't. I even visited other churches to see how they operated differently than I was used to seeing. If I was going to be a leader, I needed to see references in the areas of my leadership. It was a task I had to take on my own and I think Korey understood that. I couldn't lead like him or my brother. I had to find the texture of my own brand of leadership. That would be the biggest struggle because I rarely saw myself as someone others would follow.

I read the books. I watched others in my field. I visited the other churches, and I was still stuck on the kind of leader I was supposed to be. After all, it takes most people a lifetime to discover themselves. I was trying to figure myself out in a few months. Korey and I had been talking on and off about us having a conversation about how I would come back to the media team. The plan was for me to take time away from the team so I could learn how to be a better leader to the team by the start of the new year, but I found myself with more questions than answers the closer Christmas came. I was learning a lot about myself, and I felt less stressed, but I still didn't feel like I was equipped to go back and lead the team after a few months, not after the examples of leadership I'd been seeing during my suspension. Those were huge shoes, and I never took time to pay attention to how important leadership was until I saw it from a different perspective.

I didn't know what to do until one Sunday my brother announced that he was starting an MIT class. MIT stands for minister in training. He had been announcing it for about a month, but I never paid attention to it. I had no intention of becoming a minister. Yet, the last time he announced it I heard, "sign up". "Nah, God. Nope! Uh-uh. I'm going back to that soundboard!" I'd much rather go back to just doing sound than to join the class. I ignored the call again. Over the Christmas break, we had a party as usual. My parents would invite everyone. I'd be there until I got tired of being around people and slipped away to my studio. My brother would wait until most people were leaving before he showed up. That was our party pattern. Large crowds weren't me and my brother's thing. When he showed up, we all gathered in my parents' kitchen. Me, Mark, his armor bearer, Jay and my parents. Everyone was talking when I turned to my brother in a whisper, "so what all happens in the MIT class? What's it for?" I looked around to make sure no one was paying attention to me. "It's a class to become a minister. You learn all it takes to be one. We get deeper understandings of the Bible, go through leadership skills, mental exercises and prepare you to preach." He had already taught two other MIT classes for the church. One of which he had about 9 graduates and one he cut short because he felt the participants weren't ready. It sounded good, the way he was explaining it, but once he got to the part about preaching, I was out.

"But, I don't want to preach," my face turned up in a frown masking my fear. "Can I just write it and have someone else preach it for me?" My brother burst into laughter as I was looking around to make sure no one heard my question. "No, James! That's crazy. Preaching is the last thing we cover anyway."

"Y'all talking about MIT?" Jay, my brother's armor bearer slid next to me. "I'm signing up. You gone sign up wit me, James? We can do it together." I began laughing at Jay's Tifton, Georgia accent to buy myself some time to come up with an answer. "Maybe Jay could preach the sermon I write instead of me doing them," I thought to myself. As an armor bearer, Jay had been with my brother for about 2 years. An armor bearer would be similar to a lieutenant. It's the pastor's right hand. They saw all, they knew all, they experienced all. As a protector to the pastor, it made sense to me that Jay would be in the class. "I don't know yet," I finally answered him. "I'm not trying to preach, though." I couldn't be the only one to think that. "Why not? You could rap your sermon," my brother interjected. I didn't respond. I smiled and looked down. The truth was I saw preachers. I watched them. I didn't talk like them. I didn't act like them. I didn't scream unless there was something I was passionate about. Their language was not my language. "Well, if y'all want to be in the class, sign up this week. We have a meeting the first week of January." My brother walked away to eat his banana pudding with no bananas.

SUNDAY DECEMBER 30, 2012

After service, I met with Korey in his office again. We were going to discuss how things would go moving forward with me and the media team. At that point, they had been doing great under Christina's leadership. That was a huge relief for me. "You ready to come back?" Korey was great at getting right to the point in these types of meetings. I sat in the seat across from him on the other side of his desk and placed my hands on it. "No, I don't think so." Korey's eyes showed half surprise, half 'saw it coming'. "I'm not ready to lead the media team and I need to find out who I am away from the board." Korey smiled and nodded his head, "how do you plan on doing that?" Similar to my conversation with Terrence at Macy's, Korey had a tone that said he'd been here before. "I don't know," I sat upright. "I've been thinking about doing the MIT class coming up, but I'm not sure." Korey's eyes swelled with surprise. He paused for a few seconds, almost in pensive thought. "Wow, that's big." He was speaking, but I could tell he was still thinking. We spoke for another 20 minutes on topics that would remain private before he left to prepare for New Year's Eve service.

SUNDAY JANUARY 13, 2013

I had been getting antsy with not doing anything in church. I was never good at sitting still. Even during service, I got up at least 5 times to walk around during the sermon. I missed being on the soundboard, even though I knew I couldn't go back yet. That wasn't not all I missed. I missed being a pivotal reason why everything either went right or went wrong. It excited me as much as it frightened me. The constant movement of transitioning from one scene to another, the big moments only accentuated by the small subtle ones and the way the team functioned when we were all on the same accord. That synergy lit me up in ways too difficult to explain without being redundant. After service, Korey called me on the phone. Today we were installing a new church campus in Stockbridge, GA. The church would be called Life Revolution Church and it would be led by Pastor Alex Brown. Alex served as associate and youth pastor at Fresh Start, and he was getting his own church. We were all proud and were determined to make his installation service memorable.

When Korey called me, he asked me to come down and help the media team for the day. He just wanted me to walk their team through how the equipment, flow and transitions worked. Before I even answered I was already walking to my car headed down there.

As I arrived, I noticed that there wasn't a church building. It was a movie theater. I was too excited. Having a service inside of a movie theater was so creative to me and I was intrigued, to say the least. I saw Korey, Danny and Lace getting prepared, so I joined them. Korey introduced me to the team, some I already knew, some I didn't. "Guys, this is James. The media extraordinaire." I remember those words coming out of Korey's mouth because, at first, I didn't know who he was talking about. I hadn't done anything in sound, video or lighting for so long I had forgotten that this is what I do. It's funny how we are unaware of our skill level because from our perspective it doesn't mean much. We do things without thinking so we don't find them as special as other people do. I shook it off, smiled and got to work. I began showing the team the things they needed to do in order to have a successful service. I did the task in front of them first. Next, I undid the task and did it again with their help. Then I undid the task again and switched places with them so they could do it with my help. Last, I had them undo the task themselves and redo it for consistency. That was how I taught, step by step. For someone who thought they were ill equipped to lead, I was proving myself wrong and didn't even know it. The service went great, so great that Korey would ask me to help guide the team alongside him for the next few months, until everyone got the hang of things. With a newly found confidence in my ability to lead, I accepted. It made me happy to see someone I taught do well and I wanted to keep teaching everything I knew.

What was supposed to be a few months, ended up being weeks short of a year in that position. As Life Revolution Church grew, so did their team. The more team members there were, the more people there were to teach. Cecil and I would travel from Duluth, GA to Stockbridge, GA then back to Duluth, GA every week for a year. Cecil is an OG of the church and he's also the man who gave me my first job out of high school. He owned his own contracting company building and restoring homes. I learned a consistent work ethic from Cecil. At 64 years old, he was moving faster than people less than half his age, including me. Korey was there to help guide the worship team of the church. I was there to help guide the media team of the church. Cecil was there to guide the operations of the church. I never saw myself as a peer to Korey or Cecil. They were men I looked up to. Hindsight showed me that, in this project, I was a peer in leadership. Again, I was leading and didn't know it.

11. PROCESSING DISAPPOINTMENT

WEDNESDAY JANUARY 23, 2013

The horn blew outside my window. I jumped up and ran to the front door, opening and closing it behind me. I hopped into the truck, "What up, boi!" Jay screamed over his music. I didn't feel like screaming so I nodded my head upward, dapped him up and put my seatbelt on. We drove for nearly 30 minutes, talking about music, creative ideas and relationships. I told him about a woman I was interested in, but I never told him her name. He ran down the latest in his exciting love life. Jay rapped and we were working together to get his music out, so we were also going through a few tracks he was thinking about recording to. We arrived at our destination and jumped out of the truck in a rush. We were late for the meeting. With all the excitement of the new year and planting a new church location, the MIT meeting was pushed back a couple of weeks.

When we walked into the church, there were nearly 50 people inside. My brother was talking, and we sat in the back. While looking around, I saw so many familiar faces of people interested in becoming a minister. They were people I admired. They were people who watched me grow up. I looked closer to the front, and I saw Korey sitting with his wife, Marla. I began thinking that maybe I accidentally stumbled into the pro level AP version of MIT. I needed to be in the beginners MIT class. After another 45 minutes, my brother ended the meeting and then it happened. "Jay and James! Let me see y'all in the front please." The tone told me everything I needed to know. We walked by everyone preparing to leave and stood in front of the podium Mark was standing behind. "Let this be the last time either of you are late to this class. I will not treat you differently because you are my brother and my armor bearer. If you miss more than two classes without notifying me, you're out."

People often said and thought that there was favoritism when it came to how I was treated by my brother in church. They believed that he treated me differently. He did, but not the way you may think. There was no one Pastor Boone was harder on than me. I got away with nothing. Every misstep was caught. For the most part, people didn't even know we were brothers unless they knew us personally. At church, he was all business so it was no surprise to me that he would go extra hard on me in MIT. I nodded my head in agreement as Jay attempted to plead his case as to why we were late. My brother hit him with his ceremonial high pitched, "Hmmph" and walked away.

It was scary for me. Everything was so unfamiliar. It wasn't just uncharted territory; I was lost. I wasn't lost in the sense that I was unhappy or in a bad place. I was lost in the sense that I had no idea where I was going or what I was doing. I knew I was supposed to be in the class, but I also knew I didn't want to preach. I wanted to learn all that I could. I wanted the information. I just never saw myself as a preacher. I didn't speak like them. I didn't look like them. I didn't think like them. I had no desire to be a preacher nor a pastor. All I wanted to do was music and I was so close to getting to the place I wanted to be. I began feeling uneasy and conflicted thinking that I had to choose between ministry and music. I still had residue from my past experiences of rejection even though I knew those thoughts didn't belong to me. On the ride home, I had thoughts of calling my brother and telling him that I no longer wanted to be in the class. The only thing that kept me from calling him was the fact that I was so intrigued about the information I could learn. I was a sucker for information, and I was promised a lot of it.

MONDAY MAY 26, 1997

It was close to our bedtime and I was still watching WWF Raw on the USA cable network. We had just gotten cable TV two years ago and most of my time was spent watching professional wrestling or Xena Warrior Princess. That night, most of my favorite wrestlers had matches. The Rock, Triple H, Ahmed Johnson and Vader had matches, but what caught my attention was the final match of the night. Two of my all-time favorites, Shawn Michaels and Stone Cold Steve Austin, were a tag team going against the Hart Foundation. Howard Finkel announced each wrestler as they came out. First Shawn Michaels and Stone Cold, then Owen Hart & The British Bulldog who represented The Hart Foundation. Stone Cold and The Heartbreak Kid had no love for each other, but on that night, they had to work together. Before The Hart Foundation could get into the ring they were attacked by the unlikely duo. Once they got into the ring, The Hart Foundation gained the upper hand, being a more seasoned team. Shawn Michaels and Steve Austin were trying to win the match on their own, almost refusing to tag the other in. Either way, it was entertaining.

About halfway through the match, they realized how much they needed one another and began working as a team. They were also motivated by the rest of the Hart Foundation showing up and watching the match closely from the stage entrance. They were waiting to attack Stone Cold and HBK after the match so in their eyes, they'd better win. Already fighting an uphill battle, HBK was getting the better of the British Bulldog when the Bulldog poked him in the eye, shifting the momentum. Unable to see, HBK became a human punching bag, helpless to the onslaught coming at him. Preparing for one of his signature moves, The British Bulldog hoisted HBK onto his right shoulder and made his way to the corner. Charging to the middle of the ring, he performed his signature running powerslam. On impact, The British Bulldog pinned HBK down to end the match. The referee slid across the ring to begin his count. 1… 2… The TV turned off.

It was 11pm and it was bedtime. Mommy came and turned the TV off, "go to bed." It felt like a dagger went in my chest. Was the match over? Did he get out of it? I saw Stone Cold trying to get to him. Did he make it? I had so many questions. I needed to see the end of the episode. From my bed, I pleaded with mommy to let me see the last few minutes. It was life or death. She wasn't having it. She put the remote on top of the TV and walked out of the room shutting the door behind her. Mark was already asleep. Even in middle school, he had a full schedule. Step team, community choir and his new obsession with filmmaking had his full attention. He was out and when he went to sleep, there was no waking him up.

I waited a minute after mommy left our room and I slowly got out of bed. She and I were about the same height so she couldn't put the remote too high. I grabbed it and turned the TV back on. Using the menu button, I turned the brightness down on the TV so no one could see the glare under the bedroom door. I then used the same menu button to turn on the closed caption. If it sounds like I've done this before, I have. I muted the TV and began watching the match again. I guess HBK got loose because he just hit The British Bulldog with his signature kick move, Sweet Chin Music. Stone Cold pinned the Bulldog down for the 3 count. As the bell rang in their victory, it was short lived as the rest of the members of The Hart Foundation came storming into the ring in attack mode. Even though I couldn't hear what was going on, I felt every moment of it by reading the caption.

It may seem like that was just an intricate and very sneaky way to watch TV behind my parents back during my bedtime, but it only started out that way. I was never a good reader in school. My dyslexia flipped words in reverse order and all but destroyed my confidence to read in public. In fact, whenever we had to read aloud in class, I depended on my memory rather than my ability to read in order to complete the assignment. Our teacher would have each of us read a paragraph aloud, then defer to the next person. Once we started, I'd count the number of people before me to find the paragraph I had to read. I'd memorize it and then recite it as if I was reading in order to hide my reading deficiency.

I did that throughout elementary school and a portion of middle school. Yet, once I began watching wrestling on mute with the caption on, my reading level rose. I was gaining the ability to read aloud without stuttering or stammering over words. I could put the words in their correct order. I was gaining the ability to read and comprehend at the same time. I was even gaining the ability to speed read with full understanding. It wasn't just the closed caption that was enhancing my ability to read, it was the pace at which the people were speaking.

At sporting events, the commentators were charged with giving a play-by-play account of everything going on. Before there were televised sporting events, the only way people could know what was going on at the event was by radio. The announcer or commentator had to be skilled enough to follow the event and illustrate the event with their words for the audience to hear the event as if they were there in person. Because of that, the words in the closed caption would scroll at such a speed that I had to focus in order to keep up with it. The more I watched wrestling on mute, the stronger I became at reading. I started watching everything on TV with closed captions. To enhance my speed, I began watching sporting events at a quicker pace. Basketball, Nascar, Tennis and soccer all helped enhance my reading, but it all started with professional wrestling. Language and literature weren't all I learned by watching wrestling. I also learned geography. Every week the WWF was in a new city and state. Each time they traveled; I memorized the location. Any place where there is information to be learned, I was going to be compelled to learn it. That's always been me, so being promised information in MIT was all I needed to hear in order for me to continue the class.

WEDNESDAY JANUARY 23, 2013

My phone rang, "Ashwood!" I screamed at the top of my lungs. "What up, sis!" Jay chimed in a well. "J-Bogans! You ready for this class?" Ashley Wood, one of my greatest friends, shouted back. "Ya brother cuss y'all out for being late?" Jay and I looked at each other and bursted into laughter, "Yeah, Jay tried to explain like a dummy. It just pissed Mark off even more." I chuckled through my sentences. "You gonna have to be my church translator so I can pass!" Since I met her, Ashley had been interpreting all things 'church' for me. She knew all of the traditional stuff and had no problem educating me without judgment. The church jargon, vernacular and colloquialisms that had eluded me for so long came to me in human form. Even though she knew all the tradition, Ashley never treated me like a traditionalist. "You will be just fine as long as you don't call the 'devotion' the 'devotional'," Ashley fired back at me with laughter.

When I got home, nearly all the exciting air was sucked out of me. I was reminded of all I needed to do for my music career. My album had been re-released three months prior and I was not happy with the promotion of the company. I felt like the type of marketing and promotions they were doing wasn't moving the needle the way I desired or expected. If anything was done to move the project forward, it was done by me. I remixed and remastered the album. I provided the music video. I provided social media marketing. The company was supposed to provide the conventional marketing and from my perspective, they weren't doing their part. In our contract, there was a clause that stated if I decided to sever ties with the company, I could do so with a written request. I was preparing my letter trying to prevent myself from being disappointed. No amount of positive thinking could help me, though. "Another one for the loss column," I thought to myself as I typed my letter up. The re-release of the album was supposed to be the thing that propelled me to the next level. It was supposed to propel everyone a part of the project to the next level, and it was looking like I failed to accomplish that because I chose the wrong company to do the things I could no longer do alone. I had been doing pretty well independently, but I couldn't sustain the volume of work needed to promote me in ways that could get my work to that next level. I wasn't beaten, but I'd be lying if I said I wasn't disappointed. I finished the letter and kept it in the drafts column of my email. I went to bed.

FRIDAY MARCH 15, 2002

Like anger, my family didn't quite have a healthy track record when it came to experiencing and handling disappointment. As a 15-year-old, I had been rapping in public settings for about six months. After mustering up the courage to finally rap at the breakfast table, I had acquired a stinging reputation at school as a battle rapper. Each morning, we'd all crowd around a common area table during breakfast and battle it out as someone would beat on the table. Aside from a rapper from Memphis named Rambunctious, I was slaughtering everyone I went against. It was the highlight of my day and it's what got me up in the morning. After school one day, friends and fellow rappers, Saeed and Jeff had the idea for us all to compete in a freestyle tournament called "Freestyle Friday" at the radio station. Coco Brother of Hot 107.9 hosted freestyle Friday each week allowing rappers around the city to compete for who was the best. Even though I knew I'd be showered with social anxiety and stage fright, it still excited me to be a part of it.

Mommy and daddy dropped us all off at the radio station and we took the elevator a few floors up. Once the elevator opened, it was like I stepped into a Baby D music video. Everyone had long t-shirts on with matching air force one's, baggy Girbaud jeans with a matching hat and a gold or silver chain with matching earrings. I had on a hoodie, blue jeans and sneakers my brother bought me for Christmas. I'm pretty sure the sneakers were stylish since my brother bought them, but I had no idea. There were at least 30 of us in the room and the objective was for everyone to battle it out until there were two people left. Those two people would battle it out on the radio. The competition began and it was a melee. Each rapper cut the next one down with creative insults and word daggers as the judges looked on. Me, Saeed and Jeff looked at each other to see who would be the first of us to jump in.

Saeed lived for the attention, so he was the first. He was a half verse in before he was cut down by a more seasoned rapper. He wouldn't try again for the rest of the night. Jeff looked on but didn't step in. The look in his eyes showed that he felt outmatched by the competition around us. What he didn't know at the time was that he possessed the most captivating voice out of all of us. Skill level or not, they were going to listen to him, if he'd only speak. Stopping myself from thinking, I jumped in. I was tearing people apart. Rapper after rapper, my love for words gave an advantage that I never recognized until that point. Just when I was getting into a groove, I was promptly torn to shreds by an upstate rapper by the name of J Yung. He had a style like Cassidy as every line was puckered with vicious punchlines that made the crowd erupt in amazement. I was no match for him, and I was not chosen to be on the radio.

Jeff tried to make me feel better but all I could think about was how I came up short. It felt like I let him and Saeed down. If I would have won the competition, it would elevate all of us to the next level. We left and went back home. Daddy had been listening to the radio waiting to hear us. Once we got home and he realized we weren't on the radio, he saw the disappointment in my eyes. He went off. He began shouting about how we had no business trying to get on the radio in the first place and about how corrupt the music industry was. He went for about 5 more minutes before mommy stopped him. If we could feel worse than we did, we would have. Daddy was never particularly skilled at pep talks in the face of disappointment. From his perspective, addressing disappointment meant insulting the establishment that disappointed you and then avoiding interaction with that disappointment so that you never have to experience it again. Much like fear and anger, disappointment was too strong of an emotion for my family to confront head on.

Saeed and Jeff went home as I went into my room to lick my wounds. I laid across my bed taking the day in, and it hit me. I remember an old conversation I overheard my parents having when I was younger about daddy's aspirations of entertainment stardom in his youth. Daddy was a musician, dancer and singer with promise of making it big. He had an opportunity to dance in a commercial with Michael Jackson and it was stripped away from him by his father. I could imagine him pretending not to care and transferring all that energy to dismissing the feeling while mentally safeguarding himself to not feel that disappointment again. I could also imagine him seeing that disappointment in my eyes and it causing that familiar feeling to rise in him again thus causing him to react with such vitriol.

With that understanding, I no longer felt as bad as I did before. Instead, I began using my memory to recall the highlights of the night. I rapped in front of a lot of people and didn't feel like I was going to throw up. I held my own amongst adults, and someone came up to me and told me I was exceptionally good. Even though I was disappointed that I wasn't chosen to be on the radio, and I felt I let my friends down, I also felt a sense of accomplishment. I felt it enough that I chose not to quit, but to charge forward to see what else I could accomplish.

It also helped that Jeff was there nearly every step of the way. As one of my closest friendships turned brotherhood, our bond was forged out of like mindedness and a genuine love for one another. I still remember bringing Jeff to church with me in the summer of 2003. When we walked in, we both received the ceremonial 'who is that' look when church people saw someone unfamiliar to them and unlike themselves. We sat in the back with the rest of the teenagers who weren't forced to sit with their parents. The choir began to play a song that Jeff recognized. He stood to his feet clapping his hands and shouted, "that's my shit!" The teenagers laughed uncontrollably and the adults around us looked on in disgust. I was upset, not with Jeff, but with the adults who visibly smote him and the teens who used that moment to jest about it. Like me, Jeff wasn't churched. He wasn't groomed to be an obedient church boy. He was authentically himself, expressing his love for a song he heard with the language that he knew. He was ridiculed for it. The only silver lining was that I was there with him. The song was my shit too.

WEDNESDAY JANUARY 23, 2013

The disappointment coursed through my body as I laid my head upon my pillow. I had to remind myself, though. Me and my team created a project worth protecting and if the company couldn't see that, it was their problem. I kept all the rights to the album and could continue on without them. Battling back and forth, I fought to keep a cool head. Originally, I was going to wait until the morning to send the letter to the company, in case I changed my mind. That only created anxiety for me because my mind was made up and I was only prolonging the issue. I jumped out of bed and grabbed my laptop. I proofread the letter for the thousandth time and hovered over the send button. Decisions like those have always given me pause. Freedom and autonomy had always been my goal, yet the responsibility of it frightened me as well. Someone else being responsible for the things I didn't want to handle was easier for me because it gave me someone other than myself to blame when things went wrong. I pressed the send button and quickly shut my laptop.

12 "I'M GETTIN' MINE!"

SATURDAY SEPTEMBER 7, 2013

I sat in the car skeptical about going inside. Joe and I had sat in the car for what felt like hours. Joe went to just about every show I've ever had. I trusted him with my life, still do. He was honest, blunt and kind of a jerk. I needed that around me. Besides my brother and Jeff, Joe was the only other person that had been with me at every stage of my profession. For me, Joe was non-negotiable. Everywhere I went, if he couldn't go, neither would I. He was a bodyguard, road manager, Godbrother and asshole all wrapped up in one. It's one of the most important relationships I've ever had. I've even broken up with someone because they told me they didn't like Joe. "Whatever happened with that church we went to before?" Joe finally turned the car off and opened his car door. "Long story," I didn't feel like talking about it. In fact, I never felt like talking about it. My mind wandered while I was still in the car…

THURSDAY JULY 25, 2013

I spent half of the year focusing on myself and my music. Things were becoming easier at Life Revolution Church with the volunteer training so that was a lot off of my plate. After departing from the label, I decided to start a new project. It would be a mixtape and I called it 'The Inception'. My optimism in the face of disappointment pushed me in the direction of tailoring my project around the idea of not allowing anyone to steal your dreams away from you. I would use portions of the movie "Inception" to make my point. From the project, I had a lead single called "Takin' Over". I began performing it earlier in the summer and it caught the attention of a neighboring church. I never quite categorized my music as gospel, but faith in God had always been in my message. A representative of the church reached out and invited me to a showcase to perform. Eager to show what I was made of, I accepted.

I killed the show, if I may say so myself. Everyone at the church was amazed. I can admit that I've always had a gift of speaking to people where they were, like a human being. I spent my life making sure that I allow the people in front of me to see my humanity before they can see anything else. In the church, however, I had forgotten that showing such a thing wasn't always accepted. One of the guys from the church invited me to be on their Church's summer mixtape. I was excited. I felt as though I had finally been accepted by a world that I longed to be accepted by. I loved rapping in the church. I loved rapping to inspire people to chase after their dreams and their goals with their God-given talents. What better place is there to do that than the church?

My heart dropped the next day when I read the email. The excitement deflated out of me faster than a popped balloon. The guy who invited me to be on the mixtape sent me a message stating that they, the church, were rescinding their invitation for me to be on their summer mixtape. It was said that in my song "Takin' Over" I didn't say the name 'Jesus' enough to be considered for the mixtape. Because they couldn't find the name 'Jesus' in my song, that meant I wasn't gospel enough or saved enough. It was all getting old fast. I didn't even have any words to respond with. I was numb. Even though my main reason for creating the music wasn't to be accepted, it would be nice if someone did. I couldn't stop my mind from racing.

SATURDAY SEPTEMBER 7, 2013

"You coming or not?" Joe called out to me. My skepticism was at an all-time high. We were at another show I was invited to. A week prior, I ran into Ric Flo at the mall. Ric was a part of a duo called 'Platinum Souls'. They came to our church a lot and I was always a fan. We caught up for a while and then he gave me a flyer to a showcase that he hosted. At the time, I was excited about going to the show. After the run in with the other church, I wasn't so sure. I got out of the car and walked toward the building behind Joe. Noticing that it wasn't a church building, I felt a bit at ease. It was disturbing that I felt more comfortable and safer with the people outside of the church than inside of it. The door had a green and white star on it with words inside of it. Under it, it said "The Green Room".

Famous actress, Terri J. Vaughn opened an actors lounge for aspiring thespians to use for their acting classes and performances. On one side was a coffee shop and on the other side was a stage for performance. Ric Flo met us close to the front door and warmly greeted us. "Hey, here's my music. Who do I give it to?" I pulled out a plastic CD sleeve and a USB drive to hand to him. Some places I performed accepted USB drives, and some were stuck in the 20th century by only accepting CDs. I made sure I brought both. Ric Flo looked at my hand and began laughing. "We don't do that here, Heat." I was confused. "No tracks here, all band." I looked up at the stage and saw the band, but no DJ. "Yeah, you can let the band hear what you got, and then they can take it from there. If you want–" His voice began to echo incoherently as my gaze at the stage got deeper and deeper. I had been performing for ten years, but I had never performed any of my songs with a band. I was excited and I was afraid at the same time. I believed the experience would be great, but my song choice was the problem.

I was going to perform my latest single "Takin' Over", but the way the song was structured I needed the instrumental for maximum impact. There were adlibs and sound effects that highlighted parts of the song that brought it to life. Without those parts, it was just an ordinary song. "-- you want me to give the band your music?" Ric interrupted my thought process as he came back into focus. "Nah, I'll figure it out." I didn't know what I was going to perform but I knew it wouldn't be "Takin' Over". "Cool, I'll put you on close to the end to give you some time to think." Ric patted me on the arm and walked away.

Joe and I sat in the back of the lounge while we tried to figure out what song I'd perform. Every suggestion either of us had would be struck down by the other. It's too slow, it's too busy, it's not a performance song. After a few minutes, we just decided to stop and enjoy the show. Ric stepped onto the stage and began performing. I didn't know it at the time, but every show, Ric Flo would begin the show with a high energy performance. He was a wordsmith with a huge love for vintage 90s hip-hop. The band was amazing. Manny on the keys, Bryce on guitar and JT on the drums. They were so in sync that every song they played together felt like a concert. Ric greeted the people and started the showcase. There were poets and there were singers, rappers and musicians all coming to the stage to display their gifts. The beautiful part about it for me is that these were all believers coming together to create and present their art in a nonjudgmental atmosphere.

An artist by the name of Barclay set the stage on fire. His energy and his passion lit a match in the room that got everyone to their feet. He had a song called "Ain't No Way" that was an anthem at the showcase and Barclay never disappointed. It was also the first opportunity I got to watch mega artist 6lack perform. His smooth yet grungy style mesmerized the crowd hypnotizing them into an inspired cloud over the stage. I was so enamored with the show, I completely forgot that I still had no song to perform.

SATURDAY JULY 7, 2012

Carless, jobless, client less and an album that wasn't selling the way I intended, I found myself curled in a ball on my bathroom floor searching for refuge. I needed reprieve from everything in my life. I was going so hard so fast, and I wasn't seeing the results that I wanted. My car rides with God were happening less often and when they did happen, I didn't feel the same connection. I was overwhelmed. I was frustrated. I couldn't see the other side. I was tired. I was stuck. Each time I would gain momentum, I'd be knocked to the bottom again and I was getting sick of it. My goal was always to inspire people to chase after their dream, and I was struggling to inspire myself to get off of the bathroom floor. Every room of my house had a notepad in it. The living room, the studio, the kitchen and the bathroom all either had a notebook or a notepad in it. You never knew when inspiration was going to hit you. The notepad in the bathroom was under the sink in the cabinet. I grabbed it and started writing. My writing process included me writing down random words that I felt first. Those random words would then turn into sentences surrounding them. From there, I'd turn those sentences into rhymes.

"Bottom. Wrong. Too long. On. Mine. No sleep. Cage. My way. Guilt. Small. Tall. Victory."

"I feel like I'm in a cage that I put myself in. I want to grow, but I keep feeling guilty about rapping because I can't get it out of my head that the church told me it was demonic. That makes me feel small, but I know that I'm bigger than that. I've been convinced that what I'm doing is wrong no matter how much confirmation I get from God.

This mentally feels like rock bottom to me. I can't stay here too much longer. I've got to trust what God told me. I've gotta get up. I've gotta get mine."

Once I turned those words and sentences into rhymes, it came out like an invincible declaration:

"I've been at the bottom for too long.
So I'm headed up and I don't care who did me wrong.
Now yall know what's up, so when I tell you that it's on…
You better believe it cause I'm gettin' mine!
I'm gettin' mine!"

SATURDAY SEPTEMBER 7, 2013

It hit me! I could perform the song I wrote on my bathroom floor. I jumped up and started preparing myself. It had been a year since I recorded a reference track for the song, and I never really listened to it. I'd have to perform it from memory and then just fill in the gaps by freestyling the rest. My mouth started moving, my fingers started flicking, my head started bopping. The music from the stage was loud in the room but all I heard was me. Joe just watched. He was used to it by then. I was ready.

"I got a treat for y'all," Ric began to hype the next artist up as he did for every artist. "This man is a true lyricist from the DMV. Yall give it up for General Heat!" I walked to the stage in confidence as the crowd welcomed me as if they already knew me. I greeted everyone. While speaking I could feel my back sweating and my voice cracking. I looked behind me to the band, "Do you, I just need you to follow me." They all nodded in the affirmative. I regained my composure. I loosened the crowd up by telling them what I believed, that their dreams were coming true and they were getting theirs. All they had to do was believe. I began rapping in a capella. They listened to the chorus as if I was telling them a secret. Once I shouted, "I'm gettin' mine" they all shouted it back to me. We went back and forth until the band began to ramp up. I paused and allowed the band to vamp. After 8 beat measures, I waved them down. The room was quieted. I began rapping.

"I done been dirtied up by filth.
Beaten up by guilt.
Made to think that I'm small when I'm supposed to be standing up on these stilts.

In the night where the tears of blood that I spilt
Walls of fear that I built
But it's coming down, it's coming down
No time for you giving me the runaround."

The band came in like a surge of fortitude. I could see the sound they were creating floating from behind me into the crowd as they moved to the music. With conviction, intensity and truth, I told my story. I just didn't know that my story was their story too. I finished the first verse and waved the band down. The crowd quieted again. I rapped the chorus as the band came back. It drove the crowd wild. The stop and go in the song brought people to an understanding of how we all feel when life throws an obstacle in our path on the way to our dreams. It was relatable and I could see from the stage that it was a sentiment everyone felt. I finished the last of the song and waved the band off one last time. I stepped forward to get off the stage and I was halted by the crowd of people chanting, "I'm gettin' mine" without prompting from me. It was one of the most personal songs I'd ever written. It was a response to my own insecurity behind the disapproval of a religious mindset I didn't agree with. My response said that they would no longer have my mind. My response said, "I'm gettin' mine".

13. HER

1:13AM SATURDAY OCTOBER 26, 2013

Passing by exit 65 on i20 east, I was laughing on the phone with her. I'd been crushing on this woman for a while and was enjoying getting to know her. We'd known of each other for about 6 years but never really connected until recently. Our families were connected but we weren't. I was always the introvert of my family, and she was rarely around hers at the time. It was a wonder how we got connected at all. "Brown Man, I'm about to go to sleep! Let me know when you get home." She spoke through her 4th yawn in 2 minutes. "Oh no! We are going to eat! It's Waffle House time!" I screamed through the Bluetooth in the car. I had just come from a show where I performed so I was hungry. "You are not about to come over here just to go to no Waffle House." She didn't believe I would come. "Bet money." We hung up the phone and I exited to i285 north. Yes, I was hungry, but I also wanted to see her. Her dog barked as I rang her doorbell twenty minutes later. "Lighty My Lighty!" I yelled in a whisper like Play calling to Sharane from House Party. The door unlocked and opened but I saw no one. As it swung all the way open, I saw her sitting on her steps in disbelief, head in hands shaking her head and laughing. "I was asleep!" Her dog, Nylah was still barking as she got herself together. "You ready to go?" Full of life, I extended my hand to her. Reluctantly, she agreed, and we went to Waffle House.

Curnesia Smith was an Albany born, attitude wielding, joke telling, fearlessly opinionated country girl who fascinated me in many ways. I was introduced to her by my brother when I was twenty and according to her, I was rather rude. I don't remember the interaction, but now at twenty-seven years old I couldn't imagine being rude to her. I was nervous at the table, but we spoke for hours. We spoke about everything. We spoke about nothing. We spoke about how we were going to end up at Waffle House again in a few hours because she and Ashwood were taking me for my birthday. Ashwood and I loved Waffle House and would celebrate our birthdays together eating there. That year, though, she shared our birthday date with Curnesia. I could never get enough of Waffle House, but I also wanted some time alone with Curnesia before the celebrations began. I took her back home close to 4am.

8:13AM WEDNESDAY OCTOBER 22, 2014

A knock at the door interrupted my rerun episode of Boy Meets World as I looked out the peephole. It was Ashwood. I opened the door surprised and confused, "I need you to do everything I tell you. And with no backtalk. No questions." Ashwood meant business. She put a blindfold over my eyes and put me into her car. I was even more confused. Luckily, I trust Ashwood with my life, so I kept the blindfold on. About 15 minutes later she got in the car and began driving. I followed the movements of the car for a while, tracking where we were going, but once we got on the highway I was lost. It felt like I was in the car for hours. I was about to fall asleep when I felt the car slow down and idle. After a few moments, Ashwood opened my door and helped me out of the car, "you can take your blindfold off, J-Bogans!" The sun irritated my eyes, but I regained my sight and composure when I saw Curnesia standing in front of me with a suitcase.

I was at the airport. I probably could never replay the look on my face, I was so surprised. I didn't even know where we were going, but I knew that no one had ever done something like that for me before. "Wait!" I brought myself back to reality. "I don't have no clothes, though." Ashwood laughed as she walked towards me from the trunk with my travel suitcase in her hand. "I got all your stuff right here," she snickered. Aghast, my eyes rose as I grabbed the suitcase. It was like they thought of everything, and I was appreciative. Curnesia and I had been a couple almost a year and it had already been the healthiest relationship either of us had been in. We got each other, we loved each other and more importantly, we liked each other. I couldn't count the amount of people I knew that loved each other but didn't like each other. Even in our differences we were compatible, and we made sure we let each other know often.

Ashwood left us and we walked through the airport. Anyone who knows me knows that I'm an extreme worker. I obsessed over work with a goal of getting better and better. That's a good thing, but a side effect of it is that I never really knew when enough was enough. I was 28 years old, and I had never been on a vacation as an adult. Up until that point, I hadn't even thought about it so I was excited about anywhere we were going. As we traveled through the airport, I struggled turning my brain off work. All year, Curnesia had been encouraging me to not be so consumed with work. I was doing much better, but I still had to make a conscious effort to leave work in Atlanta. I had to mentally make sure all of my studio client work was complete, all of my writings were finalized, all of my emails were done, and all of my MIT work was complete. Ashwood was in the MIT class with me, so I was certain she'd keep me abreast to whatever happened while I was gone. My thoughts carried me through the security gate. My eyes widened when we got to the boarding gate, and I saw where we were going. MIAMI! I could already see the palm trees, hear the water crashing on the beach, Cuban music playing in the background. Any thought of me not being able to unwind and separate from work flew away fast.

PRESENT

I want to take a pause right here because this is where nearly everything in my life began to change. One of my favorite books to read has been "Outwitting The Devil" by Napoleon Hill. I read it at least twice a year. The book is a conversation Hill has with the devil about the devil's hold on the world and how he affects so many people through fear, doubt and other things. There's a realization in the middle of the book when the devil makes a surprising statement. He tells Napoleon Hill that he can no longer control him as he once did before. Something changed in Hill That made it nearly impossible for the devil to have his way with him. He was hidden, evading, and protected. Hill responded and asked the devil what it was about him that would no longer allow the devil to affect him. The devil responded, "when you found a great love in the woman of your choice, I lost my grip on you." The devil went on to explain how when Hill and his wife began masterminding every day, that's two or more brains operating towards the same goal, it pushed them further and further away from the devil's grasp. The book called it masterminding, we call it prayer. Not the prayer we've become culturally accustomed to where we beg God to fix the things we've broken in the world or ask Him to fix something that's fully in our power to fix. I'm talking about the prayer that directly connects us with God, Himself, therefore providing us an infinite intelligence to hear, see and do things far beyond our own human capacities.

We're not taught that prayer. That prayer requires confidence. That prayer requires focus. That prayer requires partnership with love. One thing I've learned about all relationships is that if the two parties are not headed in the same direction, it will not last. The devil is at his best when he has his prey alone. Any form of partnership is a threat to him, which is why the institution of marriage is constantly under attack by him. If he can stop us from committing our lives to someone we're headed in the same direction with, then he can separate us from the greatest parts of our relationship with God. Marriage isn't a piece of paper from the courthouse. Marriage isn't a wedding full of overpriced clothing, food and pictures. Marriage isn't the exchanging of rings. We created that in culture. Marriage is simply a commitment by two parties who agree to pledge themselves to one another throughout the journey of life as they head into the same direction. Anything else is culture and culture is nothing more than a societal standard made popular by a majority of people. Majority does not mean truth.

My wife and I may have legally gotten married November 4, 2016, but we committed ourselves to one another far before then. We chose each other to be the one we'd go into the same direction with. Our ideals connected, our goals connected, our passions intersected at nearly every angle. The devil may show his face around us periodically, but if we're connected and headed in the same direction, he can't get in. The moment we committed to each other; the obstacle was no longer the devil. The obstacle would now be unlearning everything he left behind inside of us.

TUESDAY OCTOBER 13, 2015

2015 was a transformative year for me in all aspects. I was honing into my true identity as an artist. I decided to stop hosting studio sessions in favor of writing more. I was operating sound & media at larger events. And I was becoming a star student in our MIT class, which had gone from 40 students to 12. My relationship with God was at a place where I trusted Him to make me a better person, but I felt myself struggling in believing certain things could happen for me. To put it simply, I'd been taken advantage of in a lot of business deals. It was so much that I considered just leaving all things business to someone else.

Because of that, I stopped believing great things could happen for me in business, in music business, in entertainment business, in any business. Each time I felt myself desiring something in business, I stopped myself to protect myself from feeling disappointed. I never discussed how I felt with anyone but my girlfriend, Curnesia, and I didn't even know how to explain what I felt. Everything else was going well, but there was this gaping hole inside of me that desired something that I wouldn't allow myself to desire.

It was almost 9pm. Bible study had gone over time, which it usually did when my brother started feeling it. That time was different, though. He wasn't even speaking. Prophetess Tonya Hall came in as a guest speaker. Highly intuitive, sensitive to God's spirit and laser focused on her assignment, she always spoke with such a conviction that made one certain that God had to be real. There was always a brash softness in her tone that said, "I love you" and "I'll beat you" at the same time. She loved people enough to correct them in a way that encouraged you if you were open but embarrassed you if you were hiding. I first got to see her in action five years prior when she first came to the church as a guest speaker. She terrified me. I was an amateur sound guy, doubtful & insecure of my own abilities and afraid of being called out. As a much more mature version of myself, she still terrified me. She terrified me in a different way. I wasn't insecure in my abilities as a sound guy nor was I afraid of being called out. Instead, I marveled at her ability to hear what God said, say what God said and still be completely present in the moment. She was an electronic surge, transporting lightning from God into a people seemingly devoid of power. The result, everyone left lit up with power. That was how powerful Prophetess Tonya Hall is.

She was closing out when she asked a question that put my heart into the soles of my shoes. "Pastor Boone, where is your brother? I need to see your brother." I wanted to duck behind the soundboard, but my legs were already walking towards the front of the church. It couldn't be me walking, my fear was still at the soundboard. Once I got in front of her, she began speaking through my entire existence.

She spoke to parts of me that I hadn't unearthed in years, and it was overwhelming. Things that I had no longer believed to be true about myself were reaffirmed. They were reaffirmed in ways that made ideas that felt old to me seem fresh and ripe. I'm certain that everyone else heard money, but I heard a level of comfort and acceptance within myself that would allow me to be my complete creative self. It was an assurance that I was headed in the right direction with what I was thinking. It ensured that I was so committed that the length of time it would take me to get where I wanted to go was no longer an issue. I walked out that night a strike of lightning.

FRIDAY OCTOBER 30, 2015

She had been fussing and pouting all day. Her attitude was inflamed because she felt that I wasn't spending enough time with her on the ship. For my birthday, Curnesia organized a cruise getaway for us and a few of our friends. It was us, Joe, Jarrod, Kenneth, Robyn, AJ, Ashley, Robin and Vedrene. We arrived yesterday and I spent most of the day outside traveling the ship while Curnesia was in the room. That aggravated her. Everyone was laughing at her because everyone knew something that she didn't. While I was out traveling the ship, I was delivering instructions to everyone who went with us. I constructed a scavenger hunt for Curnesia leading her to the top of the ship where I would propose to her. Every time she would ask someone where I was, they would shrug their shoulders telling her they didn't know. Once I got everything put together it was dinner time.

She got dressed for the captain's dinner when I said to her, "Hey, I'll be right back." The look on her face said that she was sick of me. I couldn't stop laughing inside. I went and made sure everyone was ready and everything was a go. I came back and handed her a card. I wrote her a total of 5 love letters spread out over the ship. Each love letter would lead her to the next one. Once she finished reading the first letter, the instructions told her where to go for the next one. Each letter was guarded by one of our friends with a camera in hand filming the whole thing.

Every letter revealed parts of our relationship, but she still had no idea what was going on. While she was on our scavenger hunt, I took a shortcut to the final destination to await their arrival. I was nervous. I was scared. I was excited. I was ready. Five minutes turned into ten minutes. Ten minutes turned into twenty. "Where the hell are they?" I said to myself. All the excitement was about to turn into anxiety if they didn't hurry up. I looked out of the corner of my right eye and saw a flicker of light coming from a cell phone. It was them. They were about 50ft away from me and all my words left me. Joe shouted, "sorry, we got lost!" It may have seemed like the wrong time to talk, but Joe shouting snapped me out of my trance and my words came back to me as they all approached. I dropped to a knee and gave my speech. I don't think I'll ever remember all I said, but I know it ended with, "will you marry me?" The song, 'Matrimony' by Wale was playing on my phone but the wind was too loud. It didn't matter because Curnesia began crying as she said 'yes' through her tears.

14. IGNITE

SUNDAY JULY 31, 2016

Life was moving fast and there was nothing I could do to slow it down. Curnesia and I recently had our engagement party. I just made a video for a song called "Fire In My Soul". I had just become a life insurance agent making more money than I ever had. I was dabbling in real estate investing. And I was graduating from our Ministers In Training class. I believe the phrase 'going through the motions' gets a bad rep. Those motions I went through in the class taught me more than I learned in my 12 years in public school. Every motion I went through built something inside of me that would have its day to come out. I may not have felt monumental things happening as they happened in class, but everything that happened would be stored deep into a vault that only the right moment would reveal. Over 40 people started with us in the class, yet 4 of us were graduating. That's how grueling the course was. It felt like we were on line for a fraternity or something. There was me, Ashwood, Jay and Rebecca. Each of them will always have a special place in my heart because we endured and conquered something together that no one experienced but us.

Even though I didn't put as much weight into becoming a minister as everyone else did, I appreciated what we went through to become it. That made me notice something about myself. I've never been very goal oriented, so I almost never spent time thinking about the destination or the accomplishment. I've always been a fan of the journey. I enjoyed the sweat, and the toughness of trying to do something. I enjoyed the anxiety of not knowing what's coming next or if it's even going to work out. Finishing and accomplishing were great rewards, but my rewards came from the three and a half years it took to get there. I saw tears in my fellow students' eyes, and I knew what the accomplishment meant to them, even if I didn't feel the same thing.

In my human defense, I was about to get married in a few months. I was in a transitioning period in my career path while also trying to figure out what becoming a minister really meant for me. I had no desire to preach, and I had no desire to spend all of my time in church. I'd put enough hours in it as a sound guy. Being a sound engineer opened a lot of career opportunities for me. I was able to do sound for Darlene McCoy, Wes Morgan, Karen Clark Sheard. I was able to go on the road for a few dates with Tasha Cobbs, Bri Babineaux, C West, Casey J and Kelontae Gavin. Gifted as a sound engineer, I could see sound in color as I heard it. Yet, as gifted as I was in it, I felt something was missing in me. It fulfilled me to its capacity; it just didn't fill me to my capacity. Being an artist fulfilled also, but something was missing there, too. I stood on stage next to my classmates, holding our plaques. We were all celebrating, yet my mind was already trying to figure out the next journey. I wasn't fulfilled so I needed to figure out why and figuring that out was more important to me than celebrating becoming a minister.

A minister is granted license or authority to speak, preach and teach the word of God. Although one could get licensed as a minister in 15 minutes online, religious and spiritual leaders take honor and responsibility in who they grant license to. As a licensed minister, you greatly represent those who granted you license. Because of that, most leaders take serious thought, training and counsel when it comes to who gets licensed under their name. One thing I had noticed about leaders, religious or otherwise, is that they do not take public embarrassment well. As ministers, we were also able to officiate weddings and funerals, amongst other religious ceremonies that I had no interest in. Everyone was excited and I was wondering who gave John the Baptist his ministers license to baptize people.

THURSDAY DECEMBER 22, 2016

"Hey, James! Come to my office real quick!" My brother bellowed from inside of his office. Thursday evenings were when the band and praise team rehearsed for Sunday service. It was also the time where the media team would prepare as well. Sound, lighting, video and presentation was rehearsed as intently as the music. I walked in and shut the door. "What's up?" I plopped in the chair across from his desk and tilted my head in curiosity. He smiled, "this can't be good" I thought to myself. "What do you think about youth ministry?" It felt like a trick question, "I mean, they cool. What about them?" He was about to ask a question I already knew was coming. "No, what do you think about you being youth pastor?"

A few weeks prior to the conversation, I was in the youth hallway with Anika. She basically watched me become an adult. We had known each other since I used to give her sons piggyback rides at the same in 2003. Thirteen years later, they could both give me piggyback rides while riding a bicycle. "Are you ready?" She asked. I played stupid, "ready for what?" I scrunched my face up. She played along. "Ready to become youth pastor and then after that you'll become lead pastor." She smiled facetiously as she added the lead pastor part in there. "Whatever! I ain't being nobody lead pastor. If it comes to it, I'll do the youth pastor thing, not because I want to, but because God already told me that I can either do this now or I can do it later. I'd rather do it now." To be honest, I always had a great rapport with youth. I seemed to be able to understand them beyond their rebellion and I wasn't too far gone to know what it was like to think like them. I knew the youth ministry stuff was coming. I just didn't know it was coming that fast. Me and my new wife had even spoken about it on occasion. My mind was set before the opportunity even came.

"I can do that." I answered my brother without hesitation. We spoke about it a little more before I had to get into rehearsal. I was excited about it, but I was intimidated by it. I'd be coming after who I regarded as the best youth pastor ever, Chris Cox. I'd never seen someone eat, sleep and breathe youth ministry the way he did. Now that he was leaving, there would be this huge hole that I'd have to step into. Before I left his office, my brother informed me that he wouldn't be calling the position 'youth pastor' anymore. He'd be calling it 'youth director'. It was something about the titles being taken and abused in the past. It sounded like church politics, so I ignored it. Even in a new position, I was not about to start engaging in it. I didn't care what it was called. The kids were with me. It would be announced in January, and I'd start in February. Aside from the intimidation factor of coming behind Chris, it was also overwhelming. I just got married three months prior, we just found out we're having a baby, I was now a community organizer teaching middle and high school students hip hop as a life skill, and I just turned 30. Once again, life was coming at me fast.

TUESDAY JANUARY 31, 2017

At about 9am I walked into the youth sanctuary. I technically wasn't supposed to start until the next week, but I had an idea. Over the last month, a lot of the teenagers had just been roaming around the building aimlessly because there was no youth Bible study on Tuesday nights like usual. I understood their boredom, so I began to decorate the room for a surprise start to the year. I hung colored lights all over the room, did some spot painting, and I even added a new projector. I wanted the room to look like a night club and I did just that. I wasn't finished until 6pm, that was around the time people started showing up for Bible study. I played some bass heavy clean hip hop music and turned the volume up as loud as I could stand. It drew everyone to the room. The teens were pleasantly surprised, and their parents wanted to join in. We'd spend the evening getting to know each other more and playing games before we dove into learning about their relationship with God. From my perspective, there would be no point in trying to teach them anything if they weren't comfortable enough to learn.

We developed a rhythm and a tightness over the next few months. We began building out a new nursery and bigger classrooms for our elementary school students. Something I took seriously, almost more serious than my students, were my leaders. There was nothing I could do without them, and I made it my business to make sure they had what they needed, including a break. We kept a rotation and if any of my leaders weren't available or feeling well, I'd shut everything down for the day. One thing I wouldn't tolerate was burnout amongst my leaders. Doing so, I began to develop a bit of a combative relationship with parents. I noticed that many parents were using our program as a babysitter for their children while having a diminished commitment to their child's spiritual growth. In an attempt to remedy that we started sending our babies home with a little family homework. Even though I'm not a fan of conventional school, I have a huge commitment to education. As time went along, we began to put thought into a young adult ministry. We wanted to develop a place young adults could grow, especially after graduating high school. In the first year, we were growing in so many directions. All of that couldn't possibly be attributed to me.

Upon accepting the position, Yamie came on as my assistant. Anyone who had ever known me knew that administrative work was always my downfall. Not only would it take me weeks to respond to an email, but it'd also take me months to even check it. I also struggled with organization, so the addition of Yamie and Anika later strengthened places where I was weak. If I were to get an idea, my instant reaction would be to move on it and do it at that moment. They often reined me back in so we could ideate properly. They were the ones who made what we did a success. We hosted talent shows, took the kids to baseball games for Bible study, exposed them to different career goals all while teaching biblical principles they could use in practical life. My approach was to use what they knew to teach them what they didn't. We used music, movies, pop culture and their own personal experiences to illuminate their relationship with God. It didn't matter how we did it, our goal was for them to willingly build a relationship with God, unforced and unprovoked by outside influences. I even built a recording studio in my office for my kids who were interested in making music.

I believed we were doing great until I started to notice that my kids who attended Tuesday night Bible study were not attending Sunday service. Tuesdays belonged to us, but Sundays were where everyone came together for regular service. One Sunday I was walking down the hallway to check on the elementary school kids when I walked by one of my teenagers speaking under her breath. She didn't think I heard her when she said, "that's why I don't like coming here on Sundays." My eyes rose and I turned towards her, "Jeanae!" I always shouted my kids names in excitement. "What's wrong with you?" She walked towards me and said one word, "office..." If any of my kids needed to talk to me, they knew that they could, in confidence. For the ones I developed closer relationships with, we developed a language of our own. Saying, "office," let me know that she needed to talk, so we went to my office. All conversations in my office with my kids were in confidence. I wouldn't even discuss the topic of conversation with their parents. Without giving away the conversation, she let me know that she felt she was being mistreated and judged by certain adults at the church. We spoke for about 20 minutes before I went back out to check on the elementary school students. Once finished, I made my way to the front of the church building. I began hearing adults lament and complain about the youth. They felt as if they didn't show enough respect. They also complained about some kids running down the hallways or being too loud during the service. On one hand, I had kids complaining about adults and on the other hand I had adults complaining about my kids. My automatic reaction was to defend my kids, but I stopped myself and continued listening.

I listened and I watched for weeks and months. The complaints got louder and the stories became more detailed. One Sunday, we had youth takeover, a Sunday dedicated to the youth. It was a service where all things are done by the youth. The music, the word, the ideas all would come from them. I would help out in the ideation stage, but I wanted them to be empowered to make those decisions on their own. During the youth takeover, however, I noticed that attendance looked quite different for a myriad of reasons. They all came down to a lack of support. I had never heard the phrase, "I don't do kids" more in my life and that confused me into anger. From my perspective, how could you not 'do' something that you used to be? It made no sense, but I continued to listen. The straw that broke the proverbial camel's back was when I noticed that the people who complained about the kids the most, elected to not show up for youth takeover and many of them were considered leaders of the church. That feeling I used to get as a kid about church began creeping up on me. I had suffocated it as long as I could because I couldn't articulate what I was feeling, but it wouldn't be suffocated any longer. I had an idea.

SUNDAY JULY 29, 2018

For the last month we had been promoting our upcoming youth takeover entitled GENERATION GAP. It was a service that explored each generations' differences and similarities. We chose one person from each generation to sing during praise and worship while choosing songs that reached each period in time. It was a hit with everyone and as the last song was ending, those same people thought it was over… Far from it. I prepared a talk that I would deliver before my brother got up to preach. I wrote it in hopes that I could shed light on understanding the differences in the generations without judging them. I wanted the talk to have an impact, but I had no idea how much of an effect it would have. The talk went great. It felt like a small win for unity, but that feeling about church was alive in a way that ensured I wouldn't be able to suffocate it again.

15. SUCCESSOR

MONDAY DECEMBER 31, 2018

As I was preparing to host our New Year's Eve service, I sent an email I had drafted weeks ago to Yamie and Anika. In the email, I thanked them for everything they had done for me and the youth ministry. I, then, informed them that the next school year would be our final in youth ministry. I told them we would spend the next 18 months building a system for whoever would come behind us, while also grooming whoever would come after. There was an impact that I wanted to make on people that I knew I couldn't from the current office I was in. I had no idea where I'd go or what I'd do. I just knew my time as youth pastor was coming to an end. I wasn't even sure if I wanted to stay in church. I became jaded by the rules and regulations I was expected to uphold. I couldn't just ignore the church politics any longer because they were beginning to affect the growth of a much smarter and much quicker youth than we've ever encountered. They weren't fooled by the 'do as I say, not as I do' mentality. They weren't sitting down for 'staying in a child's place'. I felt like a lot of that mentality was influenced by me, so I needed to get out of youth ministry before I began producing rebels out of my own rebellion against the construct of church.

Leaders of the church would often look to me for creative aspects of the church but would not want to hear from me when it came to things that affected change in the entire church. After I sent the email, I left my office and joined everyone in the main sanctuary. Every year we celebrated New Year's Eve differently. What was normally called WATCH NIGHT SERVICE, which I hated because of its connotation to slavery, we took the liberty to celebrate in ways that fit us. We've had 80s and 90s parties. We turned the stage into a Wild N' Out set. We've done comedy shows. We did any and everything but the conventional service. For 2018, we were celebrating by turning our stage into the set of The Tonight Show and I was the host. Our segments were wild. Our segments were funny. Our segments were powerful. Our segments were biblical. They just weren't traditional.

In between segments, we'd have little dance breaks where the DJ would play music and we'd just dance. We were swag surfing and I distinctly remember my brother catching my eye. As I stated before, my brother is a dancer. He was skilled in it and he loved it, but at that moment I didn't see the love, even as he danced. He was stiff, not just physically, but emotionally. As our pastor, my brother loved the creative things we did. In fact, he was the author of most of them, but something was changing. That freedom I was so used to him walking around with was dissipating for some reason. No one else could see it, but I couldn't help but see it. I'd been seeing it on and off for the last few months, peeking out. He'd do his best to cover it with his childlike smile, but that was only keeping everyone else happy.

As a church, we were growing in number, space and notoriety. We were trailblazers amongst the church world, especially in the Atlanta metropolitan area. Our music worship was like concerts. The church had an album and songs on the radio. We were hosting the best and most creative events. Celebrities were visiting on a weekly basis. Everyone wanted a piece of Fresh Start Church, and none of it made my brother, our pastor, happy. After a successful depiction of The Tonight Show, my brother declared the year of 2019 as a year with no restrictions while the clock counted down seconds until the new year. We celebrated. A few days later he would call me into his office again. "Hey, I want you to read this book." Sliding the book across the table, no smile was on his face. It must have been serious. If he was giving me a book, it meant he wanted me to read it ASAP. I picked it up and it was a book by Ramone Harper called IT TAKES 2. "Ok, OK. What you want me to do with it?" I inquired out of confusion at first, but once I started skimming through the pages while he was talking, it became clearer. At the end of his explanation, he tapped his fingers on the desk, "just let me know what you think of it."

I read the book the next day. In a nutshell, the book was about accepting the role as someone's number 2 in the church. Every successful pastor had a reliable and capable number 2, or second in command. Upon reading the first few pages, I knew my brother was subliminally grooming me to be his number 2. Could that be the reason I was preparing to leave the youth ministry? I hadn't even told him what Yamie, Anika and I were planning for the next year and a half. For me, there was no point in mentioning it until we had everything in place. I was reading all the things required of a number 2 and most were things I was already doing. There were qualities I had possessed. In my head, while reading, I said to myself, "I can do this." I could be a confidante. I could be a burden carrier. I could be the hammer he didn't want to be.

Then there was one word I read that changed my attitude in its entirety. Successor. A number 2 had to be willing to become the successor. That would mean me becoming the lead pastor. I closed the book and never read it again. A few days after he gave me the book, I returned it to my brother's desk while he was out to lunch. I could be everything for him detailed in that book, but I could not be his successor. Look, I had seen and watched my brother for over a decade. I've seen his vision thwarted by the disbelief in the people he trusted to bring it to pass because egos got involved. I've seen him walk into the back door of the church Sunday mornings with tears in his eyes because he didn't want to do it anymore. I'd seen every betrayal he had to pretend didn't happen to protect the reputation of someone who didn't deserve protecting. I didn't want none of that. Hell, I didn't even like church, and I certainly didn't like the community we were slowly turning into.

When we started, we were rebels. We were outcasts who built a community for outcasts showing that there was love for them and their weirdness. We were the misfits, the exception to the rule of church. In 2019, we had become the rule. The uniqueness and individuality we used to celebrate was now being looked down upon in replacement of a polished, more acceptable version of itself. We began to express what should happen as opposed to what could happen. Seeing what should happen assumes you already know the right answer. Seeing what could happen exposes you to so many possibilities you otherwise wouldn't see. From my perspective, the wonder of who God was to us began to fade and we replaced it with policy through tradition. It was almost like we were getting the success we prayed for and then prayed against it because it didn't look the way we wanted. I didn't know how to reconcile that feeling or put it into words that I could understand at the time. Somehow, I had even reverted to saying, "maybe it's just me. Maybe I'm trippin."

FRIDAY JUNE 14, 2019

Everyone met at my house. My brother called a family meeting. The last family meeting we had; somebody was pregnant. The last time my brother called a family meeting, we were teenagers. Something was up. Mommy, daddy, my wife, my brother and I sat in our living room catching up for about 2 minutes before my wife shouted, "alright now, Boone. What you call us here for?" Everyone laughed. He laughed the loudest, signifying his nervousness. Him being nervous made me nervous. He took a second and then began talking. It sounded like he had a paragraph prepared before he got to his point. Then he said it, "I don't want to preach anymore. I'm going to quit being a pastor." Everyone paused. I don't remember who broke the silence because I was so deep in thought. On one hand, Pastor is who I'd known him as for the past 20 years, since he first became a minister at 14 years old. On the other hand, I saw it coming. Pastor is all he had been known as for the past 20 years.

He was still in his early 30s and all he knew of the world was church. When I came out of my thoughts, I heard Curnesia and Mark talking back and forth. She wanted to get to the bottom of why he was leaving. From her perspective, if he was leaving to start a new chapter in his life, great. But if he was leaving to run away from something, then we had a problem. I understood that logic because my brother was extremely assertive in every other aspect of his life. The church was the only area he felt he couldn't have that same mentality. Mommy and daddy saw it from the perspective of his health, so they were fine with him leaving. I don't really think they were fine with it, but that's what they said. The more I thought about it, I was relieved. I wouldn't have to do the whole number 2 thing and our plan for exiting youth ministry could be in full effect. I told him that what he was saying made sense and then revealed my plan for exiting youth ministry. We all spoke for another hour and parted ways. I could tell my parents, mommy specifically, wasn't convinced he was leaving. Daddy didn't much care, as long as Mark was ok with what his decision was. Once Curnesia grilled him on his motive, she congratulated him. I ultimately knew the work wasn't finished, because now we needed to find a successor.

That Sunday, on Father's Day, he announced that he'd be leaving the church. I was at home nursing a back injury, but Curnesia and I watched it online. My phone blew up. Text messages and phone calls were coming from all over the place. I didn't answer, of course, but from what I could tell, it was a whole scene at the church. People were crying, walking out and in disbelief as he announced. But then something about his announcement hit different to me. As he told everyone about the transition, he said he'd be acting as Apostle while finding a new pastor for Fresh Start. Now I was still a little green on church colloquialisms, but I know damn well that quitting and becoming an Apostle are not the same thing. I was in pain and high on drugs at the time so I let it go.

MONDAY SEPTEMBER 16, 2019

I was in the main sanctuary wrapping up some speaker cables preparing for the tasks of the week. Even with so many things going on at once, I was still in an optimistic headspace. Since becoming youth pastor, I put a hard pause on my music career to focus on the kids. It was rewarding and gratifying, but I still missed music. I decided to work on a new album during the summer and I was almost finished. I called it IN CASE YOU MISSED IT. The entire album would be a voicemail sent to a friend of mine encouraging them to keep going and stay the course of their dreams. Juggling that and youth ministry had its tough moments, but it worked out. I was also preparing a sermon for Sunday. Youth takeover was coming up and I had to preach for it.

I started gaining a reputation for my preaching style. Ashwood coined me the "Ted Talk" preacher. I spoke to people as if we were in regular conversation. I didn't scream or yell unless the moment called for it, which it rarely did. My sermons were always based on the questions I had for God while reading, so I never had answers. I only had questions. I used questions to provoke people into their own thinking. I didn't want to put my ideas into their head. If anyone were to love God because of something I said, it would be of their own liberty. I'd give them the word, give them the facts, give them the stories from multiple perspectives and allow them to choose, because that's what God did for me. He didn't beat me over the head with scripture or ultimatums. He gave me the choice to love

Him. Sometimes I chose Him, sometimes I didn't. In my experiences, love always meant more and lasted the longest when it was a choice rather than an obligation. That was the mind frame I took to every sermon.

I was also gaining a reputation for not using a Bible or notes to preach. It was a big deal going around that I didn't need notes or that I memorized the Bible and my sermons. It wasn't a big deal to me because I came from a performing arts background. My entire adult life had been in music, film and theater. When it was time to perform in any of those arenas, we do not get to have notes. So, I didn't just memorize scripture or notes or sermons for preaching; I learned them and committed them to memory because that's all I knew.

While I was wrapping up speaker cables and reciting sermon points in my head, Pastor Alex walked in. We called him PA. He had been doing well and pastoring Life Revolution Church the last 6 years. He'd come up to the church every now and then to have lunch with us when he wasn't too busy. Over the years, anytime my brother was out of town Alex would be the go-to guest speaker for Sundays. The visit was different, though. We were still on the hunt for a new pastor of Fresh Start Church. Throughout the summer, we had guest speakers come in and audition for the role. They'd preach, they'd meet the people, meet the staff to see if it was a good fit for them. I loved something different about each candidate, but the one who stuck out to me was a man by the name Darius Wise. I related to him more than anyone. I loved his teaching style, and he possessed a structural organization skill that we lacked. The only question would be, 'could he be creative enough for Fresh Start?'

PA and I spoke for a while before he asked my opinion on the candidates. I gave him my honest assessment of everyone, and I asked if he was becoming a candidate. "I'm thinking about it," he smiled while tilting his head and tucking his hands in his pockets. Since we could always speak to each other candidly, I told him that I hoped he didn't. His eyes widened creating a few lines in his forehead, "really? Why not?" I stopped wrapping the speaker cables, "Of course I'd support you 100% if you did, but I know for a fact that all Pastor Boone would have to do is ask you to come and you'd do it without question. You're just that loyal a person to him. And the things you truly want to do would be cramped because you wouldn't have time for them. You want to travel and do conferences. It'll be nearly impossible for you to do that pastoring 2 churches." I felt like I said too much. He nodded his head to signify that he was listening. He was about to speak and then my brother came in, "Alex, you ready?" I grabbed my speaker cables and walked away.

Since the beginning of my tenure as youth pastor, I started developing what I thought was a bad habit of eliminating the filter from my mouth. I was always so tactical and careful about what I said, but the last few years had stripped that away from me. On a continuous basis, it had me leaving conversations and stages wondering if I said too much. That conversation provoked the title to my next sermon, SHUT THE HELL UP.

It was a sermon highlighting the full day before Jesus's betrayal by Judas. It was a sermon on how we can often mistake our misfortune for God punishing us when it's our shifted perspective. It was about getting those little pieces of hell inside of us, out of us. It was about us shutting the hell up and following through with what we knew we were supposed to do.

16. NO MORE HEAT

MONDAY MARCH 16, 2020

The news was on in Pastor's office, and we all watched anxiously. It was me, mommy, Ashley Hunter, Elder Tommy and Pastor, Pastor Alex. It was made official two weeks prior, and he hit the ground running. He was intent upon building on the creativity Fresh Start already had and expanding it. He had huge plans coming in, but the news cycle we were watching threatened to dismiss all plans any of us had. President Trump had declared the coronavirus pandemic a national emergency. The white house suggested that no one gather in groups higher than 10 people at a time. Countries were closing their borders to slow the virus down. The UFC canceled their next three events. The WWE announced they were going to host WrestleMania in an empty stadium. Nations were shutting down and we were close to being next. Covid cases were rising close to 200,000 and everyone was advised to go home.

We discussed what that meant for everyone and for the church. Fresh Start Church's mystique came from its experiences in the building. We hadn't taken the time to develop a social media footprint aside from posting updates. It was a daunting realization to not know how we'd pull off having service the way everyone was expecting. We began having conference calls every day to figure out how we'd do everything. Our first conference call revolved around producing an online service that made people feel like they were in person. Everyone agreed except me, of course. I didn't voice it, but I didn't want the same service online that I experienced in person. I was of course in the minority because in-person service didn't move me the way it did other people. For years, it made me feel weird that while everyone was jumping up and down, shouting and running around the sanctuary, I was trying to figure out what I was eating for lunch. I thought maybe I didn't have as good a relationship with God as those people. Maybe God ain't really rockin' with me like that to make me run around. It wasn't until recently that I understood I wasn't as crazy as I thought I was.

On the conference call, we scheduled to record a full service that Thursday. Everything would be all in one. We would have prayer, singing, intros, everything a normal in-person service would have. As Thursday approached, I saw my role beginning to change significantly. Yes, I've always done media in church, but I was moving into videography. Already having a history in video and some filming, I was comfortable with doing it. I would have to do it at a higher level. Once Thursday came everyone was set to go and we recorded service. Even though I wasn't exactly blown away by what we were doing, the service was good. I couldn't really trust my opinion with church stuff anyway because my expectations were much different from other people's. As a creative, I didn't necessarily need to be performed at all the time. I knew the world of performing. I knew the world of Performing Arts. Most times I just want to be talked to and have things make sense in an engaging manner. A genuinely energetic or enthusiastic personality will go so much further with the creative person than someone who's trying to perform to be entertaining. That had always contributed to my disconnect with church as a whole.

The service was finished, and it was time to edit. I would be in charge of editing video, and our music director, Tedy would be in charge of editing the audio. Tedy and I were a dynamic team. We thought alike in a lot of creative spaces, and we always wanted to push the envelope forward to a place we hadn't seen before. He was one of those musical geniuses who made creating look easy even if it wasn't. He was also a music producer, so anything having to do with music and audio Tedy was the man for it. Everyone involved was excited to see how everything turned out; so was I. I spent the next 2 and a half days editing the video. I wasn't finished editing the video until late Saturday night and Tedy finished the audio around the same time. It was taxing and time consuming, but I was gaining a new love in video editing. After working some kinks out, everything turned out well, so we continued with that model of production. The more we did it, the less time consuming it became on my part. Not by much, but every minute counted.

We were weeks away from Resurrection Sunday. In the church world, Resurrection Sunday is Easter. It's the day we celebrate the Resurrection of Jesus Christ. There were two events Fresh Start Church did every single year in a big way. There was New Year's Eve and there was Resurrection Sunday. Our plans for our in-person service were canceled because of covid so we had to think of something else. We came up with something called FLIP THE SWITCH. I didn't understand the title, but I loved the concept. For the music, the team would come up with a medley of songs anchored by Kelontae Gavin. All vocals would be recorded separately and then brought together for editing. The team would then record home videos of themselves singing along with the record and I would edit the videos to look like Brady Bunch boxes. For the sermon, Pastor Alex and Apostle Boone would tag team using various locations in the recently empty city. It was creative and it was tough, so I was all in on it. Tedy and I edited and mixed tirelessly the entire week. The result would go down as one of our best showings for Resurrection Sunday. When the service premiered live, I was asleep. I didn't stop editing until close to 4am that morning. I woke up to a phone full of text messages of people talking about the service. No one was doing what we were doing because we weren't thinking like a church. We were thinking like a mastermind.

Afterwards, we began getting requests from other churches to assist in their online productions. We were changing the way church services looked while still delivering the impact of Jesus. A few weeks later, we took it up another notch. Instead of recording our music sets live in the church, we began creating actual music videos. Every week, we were somewhere different and exciting. We built songs around the sermon series we were in and recorded the sermon in similar areas as we did the music videos. We had tapped into something so uncommon, people couldn't help but to look, whether they liked it or not. We were creating a lane and blazing a trail that others could follow suit for maximum impact. It was refreshing, but like all new things, everyone wasn't exactly on board with our new direction in worship.

MONDAY AUGUST 3, 2020

I was checked out during our zoom meeting as I walked around my neighborhood. The conversation was irritating. There were people who were complaining about our music videos, and we were discussing what we'd do about it. They expressed that they missed 'real live worship' as they called it. The claim was that they couldn't 'feel' the spirit through a music video, so they requested that we go back to recording worship on the stage in the sanctuary to feel more organic. I retorted that doing so would be a step backward not forward, but everyone else was ready to relent. We thought differently. Most people and most churches' outlook on the pandemic were to ride out the digital thing until the world opened up again. My perspective was that whether the world opened back up or not, digital was where we were headed indefinitely. Fortifying a digital footprint that we were already behind in developing was a primary goal in my eyes, not only for impact but for relevance. I was outnumbered by an overwhelming group of people and mindsets that yearned to go back into the church building. I didn't want to not go back into the building; I just knew we couldn't ignore the space we were currently in.

After the meeting and deciding that we would go back to recording the old way while also planning safe in-person services at the same time, I took a quiet drive. I needed to talk to God. It was odd because it was the first time, I needed that kind of drive in the middle of the day. I was frustrated. I could see something everyone else was neglecting to see. To not insult anyone's intelligence, I'm sure they could see it, but the pressures, chaos and uncertainty the pandemic produced prevented them from seeing the importance of it. What made it worse for me is that during that time I stopped second guessing myself. I stopped second guessing what I was thinking, seeing, feeling and hearing. I stopped saying to myself, "maybe it's me. Maybe I'm trippin'." What I heard, I heard clearly.

As a church, the universal church, we abused our buildings. Not in the upkeep or maintenance of them. We treated our buildings as if inside of them was the only place God was. Think about the phrases we use to say in times of desperation, "I need to go back to church. If I could just get to the church. You need to go to church." We didn't say, "I need to go back to God. If I could get to God. You need to go to God." The building became God so when it was taken away it revealed exactly who we were as people, as leaders and as believers. I remember pastors and church people making fun of social media and even condemning it as evil. It would humble them to find out that social media was the only way they could communicate with their people. How evil is that? I also began to notice the struggle, especially in black pastors, to deliver a sermon in front of a camera with no audience. There was no one there to scream, "preach, pastor!" Or "take your time!" The pandemic was not only revealing who we were, it was exposing who we weren't. A lot of pastors felt like they needed an 'amen' corner or a peanut gallery in order to deliver the word God gave to them in the way people wanted it. I wasn't saying that we'd never go back to in-person service. I was saying that if we didn't learn from what was being revealed in us, we wouldn't and couldn't be trusted even if we did. From my perspective we were being weak minded leaders and we had produced weak minded believers by pandering more to their emotions rather than the growth of their faith.

WEDNESDAY DECEMBER 23, 2020

I got up early because I was thirsty. The events over the last few months were exhausting, but I still believed we could make an impact on people during the pandemic. Without thinking, I drank my favorite Suja juice right out of the fridge. Something was off about it. It tasted weird. In fact, it didn't taste at all. "Shit," I thought to myself as I went to my phone to check my email and voicemail. I got tested for covid a few days prior. I had no symptoms before, so loss of taste was my first one. The clinic had just called me. POSITIVE. I immediately gathered everything I touched and took it with me as I made my way to our guest room. I texted my wife when I got settled. I was pissed. In our desperation to give people what they wanted by producing live worship sets, we were exposed and exposed others to covid. I would have to spend Christmas and New Year's isolated from my family. My frustration grew as I sat in our guestroom, staring at the walls. To get my anger out, I began doing push-ups until I couldn't move. As I laid there exhausted, I began to feel relieved that I wouldn't have to do any church stuff for the next few weeks. I'd edit whatever videos were made, but I wouldn't have to record, go anywhere or attend any meetings. That made me feel better. I didn't do well in meetings anyway. Instead, I would use the time of isolation to do something that benefited me, nothing.

I sat there all day praying or watching TV on my laptop or texting my wife. She would bring food and tea to my door every few hours to check on me. I'd have small symptoms here and there but I'd mentally fight them off. I spent half of my life in the hospital with chronic asthma. There was no way I was going to be beaten by covid. That was my mindset the entire time. Late at night, when Curnesia and our 3-year-old, Ajai, were asleep, I'd mask up and take walks outside. It kept my body loose and cleared my mind. Being stuck in a room all day, sitting or lying down made me stiff and restless. Each night I'd do something different. I rearranged the guest room, put my son's new dresser together, cleaned, I even built a studio inside the guest room while I was there. If I stayed any longer, I might have painted the place. I kept getting so many creative ideas and I could feel something inside of me changing day by day.

During the pandemic, I spent so much time focusing on everyone else. I was checking on my youth leaders, my kids, making sure the services were edited, making sure my family was alright, and I even agreed to stay on as youth pastor for an additional year while we worked through covid. I hadn't focused on James, though. I remember my wife bringing that up to me a few weeks back saying, "if you take time to focus on you, I'm going to be afraid for everyone you work with." I laughed it off, but I could feel it happening while I was in quarantine. The more I focused on the time I spent with God and with myself, I began changing. My thought patterns were shifting, my mindset was elevating, and clear decisions could be made. My decisions were:

Graduation season of the class of 2021 would be the end of my tenure as youth pastor, no matter what.

2021 would be the last year I served in media at Fresh Start Church.

I had no idea what I'd do in the spaces of those two very time-consuming positions. I just knew my time was winding down in those areas. If I'm to be honest, the time had expired. Expiration was quite the familiar feeling for me over the past few months because I was experiencing it left and right.

12:01AM SATURDAY OCTOBER 24, 2020

Ever since I decided to pursue music, I've had the same stage name, General Heat. It highlighted my yearning to be a leader and my skill with lyrics. It was a name I had grown accustomed to and even began to become. Every year since I turned 30 I would do some sort of challenge leading up to my birthday. I did an all fruit and vegetable diet for 3 months for 2020. Quarantine had me feeling like I was gaining a freshman 15 so it worked out for me. To celebrate the accomplishment and my birthday, my wife and I would go away someplace. We went to visit family in North Carolina. It always brought me peace to stay with Grace, Quisha and Jeremiah. During my time away, I'd also use that opportunity to discover what God wanted from me in the next year of my life. We would talk business, we would talk about relationships, we would talk about family, everything. As I was eating my burger from BAD DADDYS, I asked God, "So what's next for General Heat?" I nearly choked on my fries when He said, "nothing." I stopped the conversation and finished my food. I had eaten so much, I instantly got sleepy and called it a night.

I lounged around when I woke up and went outside to enjoy the weather. I wanted to get into a quiet place before I pressed God about my questions. Once relaxed and meditated, I resumed our conversation. "What do you mean, 'nothing'?" I needed clarity. What I got was an illumination. He told me the name was no longer useful and had served its purpose. The name 'General Heat' exemplified who I wanted to be, a leader with a fiery personality. That's who I wanted to be, but that wasn't who I was at the time. General Heat protected James. James was quiet, hesitant and fearful. General Heat was created to protect James from people. That's why I could be a zero-confidence, eggshell walking mute in person, but an entire beast of a man on stage. God let me know I didn't have to use General Heat to protect myself because James had finally become all of those things that General Heat was created for. It happened years ago; I just never recognized it. If I no longer needed the protection, I no longer needed the name. I understood that and I asked, "Well what name should I have?" He responded, "the one I gave you."

MONDAY JANUARY 4, 2021

I jumped out of bed, got dressed and rushed to go get my covid test. I needed the rapid test because I didn't have time to wait days for results, I already knew to be negative. When I pulled up to the clinic, a lady came to my car to administer the test. The swab reached the bottom of my eyeball and I started to tear up. About 15 minutes later, she came back and told me I was NEGATIVE. I drove off quickly. I had so many things to do when I got home. I sped to the house, opened the door, ran upstairs into my bedroom and kissed my wife. I just stayed there. All the things I had in my head to do, disappeared. I hadn't seen, felt or spent time with her in 2 weeks! While with her, I told her she'd be quitting her job soon, that year. Her eyes widened. When I left our guest room, it was like a wave of energy bolted inside and out of me. I could see clearer, hear clearer and make decisions faster because of it. Curnesia looked at me shaking her head and said, "Mmm-mm." Ajai was at my parents' house for most of my quarantine while Curnesia worked so I was anxious to go pick him up. In the meantime, I had so much energy that I decided to go rake the leaves from the front yard. Curnesia joined me and we made a date out of it. I wasn't exactly sure of what was going on with me, but it started changing everything around me.

SUNDAY MAY 30, 2021

It was my last day as youth pastor, and I wanted to do something special. Each time our youth have had a youth takeover, they would takeover using forms of worship that we taught them. For the last youth takeover, I wanted to show our youth the forms of worship that they taught us. I gathered as many of the youth leaders I could, and we made music videos using our kids' form of worship, trap music. We sang, we rapped, we danced. That was worship. We then had our recent graduate, Keturah, preach the entire word for us. My biggest joy in being around my kids was never about how much I could teach them. It was about how much I could learn from them. Ka'ron taught me that anyone could change. Talyah taught me not to be dependent on a plan B. Kamren taught me how to be confident without having to speak so much. Cash taught me that being passionate was ok. Rambo taught me that maturity isn't an age. Sarah taught me that your gift doesn't prevent you from being human. Troy taught me what evangelism truly looks like. Malaysia taught me that your surroundings don't have to infect the love you have. Jared taught me that nothing beats determination. Trinity taught me a dance is just as powerful as a speech. Corey taught me that there's a joke in everything. JaNya taught me that faith is stronger than anything.

I learned so much from so many, I couldn't possibly name them all and I was satisfied that I gave them all of me. I didn't hide who I was to seem more authoritative. I didn't lie to them to make them feel better. My goal was to teach them that their humanity was much stronger than their religion, because religion was something I couldn't give them. Our humanity is what our faith is built on and I knew that if I could get them to see that, they'd disrupt everything.

17. "WHAT IF I DID IT?"

THURSDAY JULY 8, 2021

"James, what the hell is going on at that church?" Elder Tommy screamed through the car via Bluetooth. "What's up, ET!" I responded, confused about what he was referring to. "Hold on, I got Cecil on the other line." Elder Tommy put me on 3way with Cecil. They've been the OGs of the church since day one. They were upset and confused so they came to me for answers. There was a night of worship being planned for the 17th of July and The OG's felt like it shouldn't be happening. I inquired about their reasoning and their answer made me stop driving. "We gotta be out of the building by the 1st of August!" Cecil joined the shouting. I stayed calm, but I did stop driving. We had lost our church building and it had been sold in early June. We had until the 1st of August to clear the entire building, and no one said anything to us. I was frozen. It didn't matter because Cecil and Tommy kept talking amongst themselves. They lamented the state of the church and vented out their frustrations. I remained calm. I told them I'd figure out what was going on, but I wasn't canceling the night of worship. It was the first event our youth put together on their own since the pandemic started and I wasn't going to shut it down because of poor communication that was no fault of theirs.

Pastor Alex was on vacation and wouldn't be back until the end of the month so there was no point in reaching out to him. I called around to see what was going on and where the ball was dropped. In the middle of me reaching out, I hung up the phone. I realized it didn't matter how, where or who dropped the ball. It had to be picked up. I was willing to assist in picking it up, but I wasn't going to do it alone. Either it would be done by committee, or it wouldn't be done at all. At the time, I was on crutches anyway. The work that people were accustomed to me doing, wasn't going to happen. The "James will fix it" mantra was gone. I found out everything I needed to know, went home and slept peacefully.

Was it unfair, inconsiderate and pridefully selfish to put us in that situation? Absolutely, but from my perspective, everything that was happening was foreshadowed a year prior. I allowed myself a period to be angry at how things were done. Then I was done with it. It was unrealistic to expect the same out of everyone else who was affected. The next few weeks were spent scrambling and spending money we didn't have to make everything happen. Morale was down, attitudes flared, people began leaving. The worst part about it is that the rest of the church body hadn't been made aware of anything either. By all measures of the definition, it was a shitstorm. We had a meeting when Pastor Alex got back at the end of the month to voice our frustrations. By then, though, most of us didn't have much to say, except for Teresa Bogans. My mother demanded answers. Her and PA went back and forth for a few minutes. I wasn't really paying attention. From my experience, the most important stuff in meetings all happened in the first 10 minutes. After that, we were just talking in circles. I wasn't apathetic to it. I just didn't have the capacity to take it on emotionally.

In early July, my body began breaking down. I grew up with flat feet and it started affecting me in everything I did. I was an avid runner. I ran nearly every morning. One morning, I woke up to go running and I couldn't put any pressure on my right foot. It was so bad; it took me a half hour to make it to the bathroom. It was so painful; I couldn't walk anywhere. That pain began to travel to my knee to my hip to my lower back. I didn't know what was going on with me, but I was physically out of commission.

That took a toll on me emotionally. A lot of who I am and what I do is encapsulated in my mobility. When I had an idea, my instinct was to just go do it. I couldn't do that anymore and I was having thoughts of what life would be like if I could never do that again.

While everyone was running around with the church stuff, I was researching how I could fix myself. I came across an article talking about the healing effects of long-term fasting and that led me to a book by Dr Sebi. He was known as a natural healer and his book detailed his 90-day liquid fast. It spoke about how it healed him and his mother from cancer. "This is it", I said to myself. Every year I did some sort of challenge leading up to my birthday. I'd use this challenge to reset my entire body. I started it on August 1st. That morning, I climbed Stone Mountain, bad foot and all. I went home and rested before I made my way to the church. I could help move a few things, but nothing heavy. It was emotional for a lot of people. We were moving the most essential stuff next door to the gym Cecil and I built years ago. Everywhere we looked there was some sort of memorabilia reminding us of what we were losing. There was a heaviness in the air as the truck was packed. I was walking through an empty main sanctuary and Elder Tommy came in. "You know what, JB? We really could have kept doing service the way we started at the beginning of the pandemic." Although it was refreshing to hear someone concede to a point I was making a year ago, it didn't really help us at the moment.

THURSDAY AUGUST 12, 2021

We stood in the middle of the gym, just the two of us, talking it out. I'd always been able to have candid conversations with Pastor Alex. It would currently be different. I had to tell him things he didn't like and things he may not have seen. I told him about how people were feeling about the last few months and how that lack in communication contributed to people's frustrations. It's one thing to not say anything when nothing is going on. It's completely different when there are multiple things happening and nothing is shared. I understood the pressure he must have felt coming after my brother as pastor. I didn't envy it at all. I also didn't want him to drown in those expectations that didn't belong to him. There was no way he could be Pastor Boone. At the same time, there was no way anyone else could be Pastor Alex. I mentioned that I believed that Pastor Chris was the best youth pastor I ever saw. A lot of that was because he had Pastor Alex to piggyback off. As a brother, I saw Pastor Alex sinking into a prided hole of comparison under an unfair pressure of meeting someone else's expectations.

I went home that night encouraged. I told my wife that I felt like he really heard me this time. We had been praying for him for months and we wanted him to succeed. We also knew that he wouldn't be able to until he was completely him, freed from the things that didn't belong to him. That's true for all of us. The next week, Ashley and I were at the gym looking through some things that we needed, and we got an idea. We could turn the gym we were in into a sanctuary. It was big enough. It just needed some work, a lot of it. We both cleared our schedules and began putting it together. We moved everything, we painted the walls, installed a sound system and put the chairs down. We were initially planning an in-person service for outside of the gym, but since we built us a sanctuary, we could have it inside. Ashley and I left that night exhausted.

Tory, Tim and I came in on Thursday, the day we record service, and tension was high. The gym was quiet, PA was in the back and Ashley was in the front. Tim walked to the back where PA was, and Tory and I set up the cameras. Ashley walked over, "He didn't even say thank you, ungrateful ass!" It was said under her breath, but I could hear her clearly. "Whoa, whoa, Hunta. What's wrong with you?" I asked as Tory started to laugh. "He didn't even say thank you for setting up. He just came in talking about how we gotta fix the holes in the walls." Ashley had a full light skin Athens-bred attitude. I calmed her down for the moment, but I could also see that it was a lot of pent-up frustration from her experience. Ashley had been doing just about everything. She was admin, graphic designer, social media manager, new worship leader since Tedy left and her salary had been cut in half. The ungrateful slight was just what she saw in front of her at the time. She was already a ticking time bomb. PA eventually came out and thanked us for what we did, but the damage with Ashley had already been done.

WEDNESDAY AUGUST 25, 2021

"I was trying to get here before anybody showed up." My brother walked in the gym as I was preparing for a recording. He sat down and we talked for a while. He spoke about how he was thinking about just dissolving the church. When he said that my heart dropped to my knees. He was disheartened at the recent events and expressed his feelings about them. I told him that most people are just holding on waiting for him to make his return. "And that's not happening." We both said and laughed at the same time. "Maybe everything has to be broken down before it can be built back up." That was a sentence I was getting tired of saying aloud. It was my perspective that maybe God wants to tear the whole thing down so He can build something new, something stronger. It was also my perspective that the longer we kept trying to hold onto what we had, the longer it's going to take to build back up. "I don't know, but right now I'm just thinking about shutting the whole thing down." He left before anyone else showed up.

3:06AM THURSDAY AUGUST 26, 2021

"Nope, nope! Not doing it." That was me, pleading with God not to have me send the text message. I hadn't eaten in just under a month, so all of my senses were hypersensitive. The pain in my foot, knee, hip and back had gone completely. And God's voice was the loudest thing in my ear. He woke me up a little after 2:30am. I wrestled the covers to go back to sleep. Nothing worked. I knew what God wanted, but I just wanted to go back to sleep and deal with it later. 3am and any chance of me going back to sleep was fading away. "I don't want to!" I sat up on the side of the bed, stood up and took a walk to the bathroom. Walking back to the bed, I noticed that there was absolutely no pain in my body. I began walking around the house. I was grateful and gratefulness was often expressed in obedience, in my experience. I sucked my teeth, grabbed my phone and went to my text messages. "What if I did it? The church…" I quickly closed my phone and shut it off, I was so uncomfortable.

My brother had approached us before about being pastor of Fresh Start back in 2019. Curnesia and I immediately shut it down. "I ain't first lady material!" She shouted across the dinner table. "First Lady? Shiiiid, I ain't Pastor material." I responded. We wanted no parts of it. I lost my trust in the construct that the office represented, and I knew I would never fit in the community of pastors. The only reason I considered it was because God wouldn't leave me alone until I did. I watched my brother for years enter the back door of the church with tears in his eyes on Sunday mornings. I witnessed the burden on his shoulders, the necessary one and the unnecessary one. I saw people treat him like he was their savior and their property at the same time. Boone was more important to them than Jesus, no matter how much they expressed otherwise. I didn't want any of that and if those attributes were the recipe for a successful pastor, then I would certainly be a bad one. I walked around the house for a while. "It's out there now. He can always just say no," I said to myself as I got back in the bed to stare at the ceiling for a few more hours.

12AM SUNDAY OCTOBER 24, 2021

Luckily, we hadn't spoken about the text message since I sent it. Maybe he didn't want me to do it. Maybe he's going to dissolve the church. Maybe he's going to go back and do the church. Either way, I did my part. I could rest in that. Meanwhile, it had been 85 days since I had eaten any food. My body had completely changed. I went from weighing 230lbs to weighing 170. My mind was working 10 times faster. I had a resting heart rate of 47. My limbs were more fluid. I felt no pain. My spirit was clear. I didn't just feel like a new person, I was a new person. To celebrate, I got meals from two of my favorite burger places, 5 Guys & Bad Daddies and I waited until midnight to eat them. It was an emotional journey. I learned things about myself that I never would have known otherwise. I felt like I could take on anything, I could do anything. I felt invincible. I made a documentary of my journey because my 85-day liquid fast healed parts of me that I didn't even know were broken. It was a generation changing experience. I would recommend it to anyone seeking a transformation. I warn you, though, if you do not have a good enough reason to do it, don't. It is not for the uncommitted.

TUESDAY NOVEMBER 23, 2021

After getting back from a filming gig in North Carolina, I called Pastor Alex. He had texted asking to talk. I assumed he wanted to discuss how the next in-person service was going to go. To my surprise, we didn't discuss that at all. He expressed how he was seriously considering letting go of preaching altogether. He said he'd be announcing his departure from Fresh Start at our next in-person service. "Me and Apostle Boone was discussing possible replacements and I told him that I couldn't think of anyone in that spot but you." It had been nearly 3 months since we first had the conversation. I told him that my brother and I discussed it a week prior before I went out of town. We discussed how he wanted to do everything, and we got off the phone. I could feel his discomfort. Pastor Alex loved Fresh Start. It was his home. It was where he was groomed as a pastor. To the core of him, all he wanted was for Fresh Start to thrive. That fact is undebatable.

SATURDAY NOVEMBER 27, 2021

"What the fuck have I done?" My wife laughed at me listening to me talk to myself. "I can't be nobody pastor. What am I doing?" Everything in me wanted to call my brother and tell him, "Psych! I was just playing. I don't want to do this no more." Curnesia stopped me, "James, what do you want to do?" "I want to help people find the most creative parts of themselves. I want to help them understand their relationship with God without the confusion of the religion niggas made up." Those sentences summarized what I wanted to do my entire life. "That sounds like a pastor to me." She responded. "Yeah, but I want to do it with art!" I exclaimed. "Then, do that. You the pastor, right?" She walked away. "You can't just drop the mic and walk away like that!" We both laughed and I began shooting text messages to a few people I saw being a part of it that hadn't already left.

7:07PM WEDNESDAY DECEMBER 15, 2021

I started the meeting by thanking everyone for being there. Everyone knew I didn't do meetings, so they knew it was pretty important if I was calling one. I didn't waste any time. I told everyone at the beginning of the year I'd be taking over as lead pastor of Fresh Start. Everyone's eyes looked the way I felt. "Oh shit, I just said that out loud." I grabbed my chest and everyone laughed. It was the first time I said it aloud. I texted it before, but I never said it. "It hit different, saying it, huh?" Kali laughed as she spoke. It did. It felt like I needed to sit down. I continued the meeting letting everyone know what I saw the church being and how honored I'd be if they joined me. I was very clear that we would not be popular for a long time, if at all. We'll be pointed at, made fun of, chastised and ridiculed. I also made it clear that it may come from people that they loved and admired. "There will also be people who start out with us and be like, 'yeah that's cool'. Then as time goes along, they'll want that old thing back. We always desire the familiar because it makes us feel the safest. And they'll leave us. That's fine too." It was important that I was forthcoming and completely honest. "Then, there will be the people who just have to see it happen for them to believe. It may take a few months. It may take a year, 3 years or 5 years. They may leave and come back. That's fine too." The road they were taking, should they choose it, wouldn't be for the fearful, the hard hearted nor the people pleaser. I felt it was wise that they knew that from the beginning.

12AM SATURDAY JANUARY 1, 2022

My phone was vibrating like crazy. We had put together an online experience for New Year's Eve that highlighted our proudest moments of 2021. We'd have a word by Pastor Alex and then the announcement by Apostle Boone. I sat by my computer nervous like I didn't already know what was going on. I already knew that most people were tuning in just to see if my brother was making his return to the church so they could come back. I always thought that was pretty funny. It only became unfunny when I realized most people were using him as a middleman for their own faith. Once the broadcast was over, I had to turn my phone over on its face so I could talk to my wife. "James…I'm not puttin' on no damn hat!" We both laughed. She had been saying that nonstop since the conversation first came up. We had a long conversation about me taking my time. I was excited to hit the ground running, but I knew she was right. I couldn't afford to burn myself out, especially doing something I'm so ignorant of. I had just become the pastor of a church. I didn't know anything about the inner workings of a church. I'd be learning as I go. I was usually ok with that. I can go full speed ahead and fall on my face, get back up and keep going. This time around, I had people following me who aren't a glutton for punishment like me so I had to be careful as well. The nuances were so detailed, it could make your head spin. Even though I had less than a month to prepare, I was ready for whatever may come.

18. LITERALLY,
A BAD PASTOR

WEDNESDAY JANUARY 12, 2022

I had this eerie feeling of nostalgia as we entered the chatroom for the appointment. Curnesia was calm, but I was agitated, and I didn't know why. Over the last few months, we'd been getting our son, Ajai, evaluated to determine if he was on the autism spectrum. Lack of eye contact, speech delay, socially awkward were words that triggered memories I had long forgotten. We were speaking with Ajai's psychologist, and everyone's words started to sink into a tunnel where sentences, parts of speech and even inflections were mixing and matching the same mood and tenor as the doctor's appointment with my parents and me 30 years prior. I wanted to scream, "I will burn this whole motherfuckin' hospital down," like daddy did but I didn't. It was my own personal time trip and there was nothing I could do about it. They graded on 3 levels of autism. Level 1 the child would need very little assistance. Level 2 the child would need some assistance. Level 3 the child would need a lot of assistance. It was determined that Ajai was what they call autistic 2 because Ajai wasn't speaking.

I didn't respond the way my father did because I was confident about my son. He wasn't normal and he wasn't supposed to be. Nothing in my mind or body would ever desire for him to be normal. He was exactly who I prayed for. He was exactly who I named.

MONDAY JULY 17, 2017

We had been arguing over our son's name since I told her she was pregnant. Yes, I told my wife she was pregnant before she ever noticed. She took about 4 home pregnancy tests and went to the doctor before she believed me. Nearly 8 months we had been arguing about what our son's name would be. I wasn't budging. I decided that his name would be Invincible. Invincible Marquis Bogans. Curnesia argued me down for months, begging me to not let this be her child's name. "I do not want my baby getting bullied in school cause some lil asshole wants to try and see if he is really invincible." I responded, "Our son is going to be mixed martial arts trained. I ain't worried." For every point she made, I had a rebuttal. "My baby got to get a job," she said. "My son will be a business owner," I responded. She even tried to get other people to convince me to change my mind, no dice. It went on for months. My son's name was a hard line for me, and I don't have many hard lines in my life. A hard line is a stance, ideal or emotion that is immovable no matter what. We learned that in therapy.

Finally, she texted me while I was working. She had been on bed rest for a while because our son was draining her amniotic fluid. In a last-ditch effort, she sent me some more names. In parenthesis, her text stated, "all of these names mean INVINCIBLE in a different language." I looked at the list, intrigued. "Aerowyn, nah... Carney, sounds like a carnival, nah. Colson? Sounds like a white boy that won't stop talking. Next. Nichaela. Sounds like I'm trying to get him dual citizenship. Nah." I was about to close my phone out when I saw it closer to the top of the list. Ajai. It's an Indian name originating in Sanskrit meaning 'unconquered', 'unsurpassed', 'invincible'. "That's it," I screamed in my office. I sent it back to her and she was overjoyed. That was good to her, but more importantly, our son wouldn't have the name 'Invincible' outright.

WEDNESDAY JANUARY 12, 2022

I've always had a special bond with my son. It was more than a father and son bond. It was like we always understood one another. We've got our own language. So, whatever the diagnosis was would never have enough strength to overpower someone who is invincible.

7:07PM WEDNESDAY JANUARY 12, 2022

I prepared a dinner for the ministers and elders of the church for the week after my first meeting last month, but I had a covid scare and ended up not being able to attend my own dinner. I made a video for them announcing to them what would be happening so they wouldn't find out when everyone else did. I was able to schedule a formal meeting with them in-person. It was important to me to see them and hear them out. For the last year and a half, they've had no voice and were out of the loop for much of our time in quarantine. I began the meeting with prayer and then I opened the floor to them. The things I needed to say would only take 7 minutes tops so I yielded, to them, the floor immediately. I let them know that Kamari and Asha were on Zoom taking notes and they had my utmost confidence so they could speak freely. No one spoke for the first few minutes.

I had been hearing grumbling all year from all different sides, so I knew they had something to say. They just had to feel comfortable enough to say it. I waited. I didn't speak. I didn't poke or prod them. I waited. "Well, I have something to say," one of our newer ministers spoke. The content of the meeting was privileged so the things that we said won't be divulged, but once one started to speak the floodgates were open. Asha, Kamari and I developed a schedule we would go by in the meeting but judging by the responses we weren't going to get anywhere until the air was cleared. Kamari was texting me that it was time to move on, but we couldn't. After each person spoke, I asked, "anyone else?" I wanted everyone to speak. I felt the frustration emitting from them. I knew it wasn't my place to fix it, but I also knew they hadn't had a place to put it. We continued. An hour and a half passed, and we were down to the last person to speak, my wife. I can say this because she's my wife, but she lit into the church's ass. She made sense, she wasn't biased because she was my wife and she expressed how she truly felt. That was a catalyst for some people to have a round two and say all of what they truly felt. I welcomed all of it. About 15 more minutes passed and I asked again, "anyone else?" The room fell quiet. I only heard breath. "I want everyone to know that everything you've said is valid. Everything you feel is valid. I also want you to know that the way you've been feeling for the past 2 years, I've been feeling for the last 7." Shock filled the room. In all honesty, I've felt that way all my life. I just didn't want to be dramatic.

Before my current position I was a career sound guy. I ran sound for countless churches. As a sound guy, you got to see everything without intrusion or distraction. I watched how people came into the church Sunday after Sunday, going to the same seat, not speaking to anyone they didn't think was important. I watched the same person shout for the same reason each Sunday with the hopes that someone would fix something in their life that they could fix themselves. I watched people sit next to the same people every Sunday and still not speak to them. I also watched people place the burden of their faith and salvation on the pastor to absolve themselves of responsibility. I watched people walk into the church, sit in their seats, look at the choir and say, "entertain me. Sing my favorite song so I can feel the spirit." I watched praise team singers use worship as their therapy session, bleeding all over people. I watched preachers' need to be loved taint the very words that come out of their mouths. I watched preachers use their platform, the pulpit, to attack people rather than the spirit that's attached to their target. I hate church. I hate what we've created it to be. I hate how we've made it an exclusive club people can get into based on behavior qualified by us. And then those qualifications change based on what culture is doing. We had abused our churches because of the power it yielded and then felt justified in doing so. We made it an emotional concert using Jesus' name to hide the fact that we don't study our word or nurture our own relationships.

I told the ministers and elders things about me that they never knew. Some of them had known me for a decade. I assured them that I was committed. I also assured them that what we're doing wasn't easy nor was it going to get easier. I left the lines of communication open, not only for me, but did each other as well. After the meeting I was exhausted. I knew I left so many things out that Asha, Kamari and I put on the list to discuss, but the meeting was an indication that moving fast wouldn't be beneficial to everyone. People needed to heal. As a church, we had lost trust with our community and there was no certainty that we'd get that back. There were so many layers that I was finding out about, it was overwhelming.

We started our online services in the beginning of January. I made my home a recording hub. One room was for audio and the garage was for video. I painted a green screen on the wall to aid our music videos and build surroundings for my sermons. Every month would usher in a new sermon series based on a different subject. Our very first sermon series was called CHURCH IS DEAD. I believed that the church as we knew it was dead, and rightfully so. The methods and models we had used for the last century ran its course of effectiveness. We clung to it out of familiarity and comfort. Every quarter-generation, life as we knew it changed. Everything around us changed, we changed. Everything except church. I wanted us to begin to ask questions, the questions we were yearning to ask but didn't. I believed that any faith strong enough to be able to withstand a cross-examination of honest questioning was a faith worth believing in. I came to find out that the faith of Jesus was strong enough for that, but the construct of church we created was not.

My questions ran deeper and deeper. I had more questions than answers. I questioned how we even measured success in a church. Some say it is about the amount of people we get saved. That made me question how we measure people getting saved. How do we decide who is saved or not? What gives us authority to determine salvation? If salvation is a personal decision, where one says with their mouth and believes in their heart that Jesus is Lord, how do we, from the outside looking in, get to determine and number who was saved? When I was a youth pastor, I used to hate doing the call to salvation at the end of service. We would tell everyone to stand, and if there was anyone who wanted to be saved, we told them to come to the front. What if someone doesn't want to come up to the front? What if someone has social anxiety? Why did we try to make a public spectacle of salvation when salvation was a matter of the heart?

Some say church success is about the number of members you have. During that same call of salvation, there would also be a call for anyone who needed a church home. So, we based our success on the number of people we could convince to become a member of our community. You know, for a church culture that had summarily lamented and debased the social media culture, their metrics of success are quite similar. I even began to question the cultural differences in churches. That was where I got disturbed. I noticed something about other cultures, white, Asian, Jewish, etc. Their churches were built on things like trusts, inheritance and insurance. For the most part, our black churches had been built off tithes and offerings. That, therefore, made every single move that the church made dependent on the giving of the people that they were serving. It would then handicap that leader or that pastor by forcing them to cater to people's emotions in order to make them more comfortable, excited or convicted to give. If that's what I would have to do to keep a church going, we were going to be poor.

I filmed an event years ago at a large church. They had guest speakers come every night. A popular guest speaker was scheduled for one of the nights. The speaker and the pastor of the church were in the pastor's office, speaking before the service, going over everything. The guest speaker said to the pastor, "hey, when you go out there before you call me up, do your offering." The pastor said to the guest speaker, "Well, we usually do an offering at the end of service." The guest speaker responded, "trust me, do it this way. I do this. Ask for your offering before I go up. When I go up, I'll do my thing and get you another one. It works every time. I guarantee you." I felt disgusted. Is that what we really do to the people we're supposed to serve? I wholeheartedly believe in giving, but to give means to present voluntarily without the expectation of compensation. We had convinced people that if they give, they'd be compensated with something. That isn't giving. That's an exchange, a transaction, a trip to the grocery store.

Our first month of services addressed those topics and others in our CHURCH IS DEAD series, deconstructing everything we believed about church in order to leave nothing left but the truth. I believed that seeing the truth, good, bad and ugly, would put people in the best position to choose if they wanted to love Jesus. We started out on fire. Month after month we were pushing the envelope more and more. We were receiving some really good feedback, but then Easter season came around.

MONDAY APRIL 11, 2022

I woke up to an email. That was my first mistake. The first thing I did in the morning should not have been to look at my phone. I was being notified that the church didn't have enough money to pay our staff. I was also notified of charges to the church's account that no one was aware of. Between yearly subscriptions we weren't using anymore and oversights, we were in a bad position. We were planning on hosting a gala for our members for Easter, but the current events ensured that was not going to happen. That was a part of church business I was ignorant of. I didn't know how to fix it. I was told that people weren't giving, and more people were leaving to go elsewhere. Covid was rapidly moving out of the news cycle on the heels of the conflict with Russia and Ukraine. That meant more churches were going back in person for service. Not us. We had no building anymore, and even if we did, that's not what I was instructed to do. I felt responsible for the 'people not giving' part. I felt like I asked for that. I encouraged people to only give if their heart was in it. It had to be their choice. I was now seeing that a great number chose not to.

We powered our way through. Instead of doing a gala, we joined Elder Tommy's organization FEED MY PEOPLE and we gave out meals Easter weekend. We also sponsored a gas giveaway. I felt that was far more impactful than the gala. Gas was almost $5 a gallon at the time. I was thankful that we were able to pivot and maneuver, but I'd be lying if I said I wasn't frustrated. I was frustrated that we were being affected financially by actions that were made years ago. I was frustrated with myself for not seeing it ahead of time. I thought we had far more flexibility than we actually had, and I didn't see it. Even though I felt the gas and food giveaway was impactful, there was a part of us doing it that I didn't enjoy. While we were handing out gas cards and pumping people's gas, I felt weird while I was filming it. The fact that I was filming it made me feel dirty. Somehow, giving turned into showing everyone else that we were giving so we could be seen. That's what it felt like and I didn't like that feeling. I thought about how I would like it if every time someone gave me a gift, they filmed it for everyone to see them giving the gift. It felt demoralizing and a bit inhuman. From then on, no one would know we were giving to our community except for those we were giving to and those doing the giving.

WEDNESDAY MAY 4, 2022

My wife and I went away to Panama City Beach, FL for the week. We both needed it. We were neck deep into new ventures and to be perfectly honest, we were getting our asses handed to us. We chose to get away from it all while we could. I began getting calls and being asked, "when we were getting a building. When can we have an in-person service? Other churches are back in person. Covid is over. If this doesn't change, I'm leaving." It was tough. I wasn't eating properly. I was gaining weight. We had to let go of our staff. I was stressed and I was angry. I began to question myself and my resolve. I was sure of what God told me to do, but it didn't look like it was working. I really felt like a bad pastor. "Maybe I heard wrong. Maybe we do need to go back in person. Maybe I'm trippin'." As soon as I said the last sentence to myself, I snapped out of it. It has always been my pattern to question myself or think that I'm trippin' when I see something other people don't. I had to choose whether I was going to abide by what I saw or by what others saw. Those choices sounded easy enough, but they didn't feel easy.

I was sitting on the balcony watching the sun come up. It was time to have a long conversation with God, unencumbered by distraction. I needed to know why He had me in this situation and I had time to listen. I sat there waiting for God to speak, nothing. I meditated to clear myself and still nothing. "What's going on?" I thought to myself. "Why can't I hear from God?" I started to get nervous. I sat there a little while longer. The blue hour was turning into the golden hour, and I was losing patience. I began listening to some music on my phone. I was skimming through some of my old tracks looking for one in particular when I came across a song I did called "One By

One". The song sampled the artist Enya and in the beginning of it I quoted 1 Peter 5:6,7. It said:

"Therefore, humble yourselves under the mighty hand of God, that He may exalt you in due time, casting all your care upon Him, for He cares for you."

I was so busy trying to get answers from God and He was trying to get me to talk. I chuckled a bit and repositioned myself in my seat. "What's really bothering you?" I heard Him loud and clear, but I wasn't ready to answer that question. I didn't know what was really bothering me, so I just started talking. The more I spoke, the more I understood what was going on. I was angry about what I inherited and the condition it was inherited in. It was like everything was dropped off at my doorstep and everyone left before I could open the door to see everything inside. I remembered when I first became youth pastor, and I was told that the church board didn't want me in that position. Now, I'd been pastor for nearly 6 months, and I hadn't had one meeting with the church board. I was angry that I was isolated. I was angry that I was too stubborn to follow along with what everyone else was doing. I was angry that everything wasn't working the way it was shown to me. I was angry that God would even put me here knowing damn well I don't like church. I was angry that I was committed to it. Otherwise, I would have already quit.

I couldn't hear God before because all I could hear was my own anger. Once I got all of it out, His voice got louder. He was telling me that he wanted to build a new Fresh Start and that old Fresh Start had to be burned to the ground as an offering to Him. The old mindsets, the old ways of thinking, constantly wanting the old thing back. It all had to be burned away, and the last part of it that needed to be burned was the part inside of me. I was there from the very beginning so naturally there would be parts that I'd be holding onto and not even know it. Fresh Start Church had been giving people fresh starts in their lives for 13 years.

Now it needed one of its own and no one could get in the way of that, no matter how much they wanted the old Fresh Start back. I finally understood what I was there for. God told me to isolate myself. Preach the word but isolate. If I was going to build something new, everything old had to be gone.

PRESENT

I must admit that isolating was and is tougher than I anticipated. I wanted to engage with people about what we were doing. I wanted to see people. I wanted to get feedback, but I was also tired of not listening to God. Isolating allowed me the space to know my purpose in my current position. Isolating allowed me to write this. Isolating helped me to hear clearer. When we got back from Panama, I was changed again. I've personally done more elevating in the past year than I have in the last 30 years of my life. I'm elevating and I'm elevating quickly. I don't know when I'm going to be let out of this space of isolation, but I'm confident in what's going to come out of me when I am.

I believe there's a place for creatives in our faith, even if we don't think the same way others do. We speak differently. We emote differently. We behave differently. We're often deemed as inappropriate according to some, but we belong the same as everyone else. We can no longer be the ones called on when our gift is needed but humanity isn't. We can no longer be forced to fit into the long-established mindset of church decorum. And we can no longer minimize ourselves because we've never seen anyone in the spaces we're meant to occupy. Our faith doesn't have a face. It has a spirit and we're a part of it. No one can take that away; they can only cause us to take it away from ourselves.

To my family, friends and loved ones, thank you. To those who left, thank you. To those who stuck around, thank you. To those who will be there in the end, thank you. To each and every pastor; The work of your office is tough, but it is not as tough as you have been led to believe it has to be. You are not God to your people, nor do you have to be. You are not their answer, you are their leader. The self-induced stress is not a part of the mantle. It's a societal handcuff that says you must be something for someone that they don't have to be for themselves. You will not succumb to a world or a people that has higher expectations for you than they have for themselves. That is not your responsibility. You are loved, you are appreciated and your space as a human being is to be respected.

There. That's the end of my Ted Talk.
Signed,
Bad Pastor.

185

AFTERWORD
By Curnesia Bogans, LMFT

I've watched you laugh. I've watched you cry. I've watched you be sad, and I've watched you glean with joy. I've seen you afraid. I've seen you bold and fearless. But to literally watch the promises of God fall on you like never before has been the greatest gift to observe. 2014 you and I fasted and prayed together as a couple for you to learn God's voice. To now see how God not only speaks clearly to you but also uses you as His voice to teach and preach His word to others is more rewarding than you will ever know. Baby, I'm beyond proud of you for sharing yourself with the world in ways that weren't always easy. The sleepless nights. The sacrifices of time and attention to yourself. The heavy days of you carrying the spiritual weight of others in the midnight hour. All these things are the makings of you. I'm honored to be your wife and I am excited to see what's next along the journey. If you are the definition of a bad pastor, may you inspire others to be just as bold and bad as you. I love you, baby. Continue to give hell a reason to work harder than the average opponent. I'mma ride with you until the wheels fall off, and then some! Thank you for trusting the gift to be a gift.